POP/ROCK SONGS

ISBN 978-1-4950-0258-8

HAL•LEONARD®
CORPORATION

7777 W. BLUEMOUND RD. P.O. BOX 13819 MILWAUKEE, WI 53213

Visit Hal Leonard Online at
www.halleonard.com

ABRACADABRA

Words and Music by
STEVE MILLER

Moderately

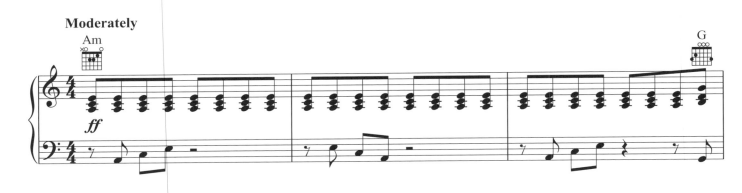

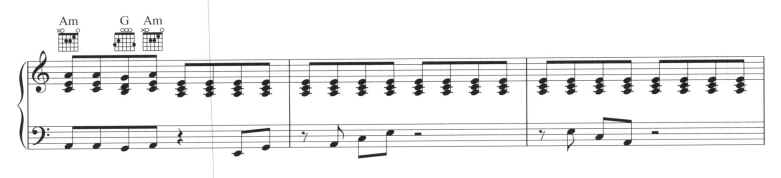

I heat up, ___ I

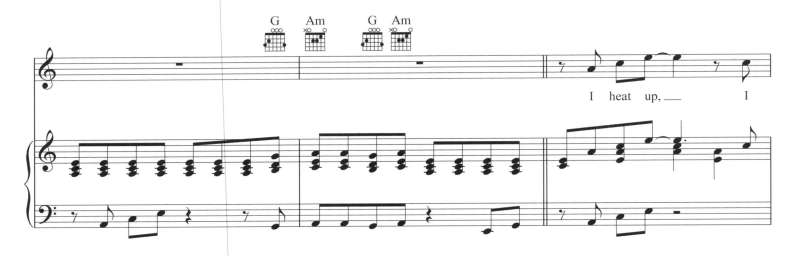

can't cool down. You've got me spin-nin' a-round and 'round. ___

'Round and 'round ___ and 'round it goes, ___ where it stops

no-bod-y knows. ___ Ev-'ry time ___ you call my name ___

I heat up ___ like a burn - in' flame. ___ Burn-in' flame ___

full of de - sire. ___ Kiss me, ba - by, let the fire ___ get high - er. Ab -

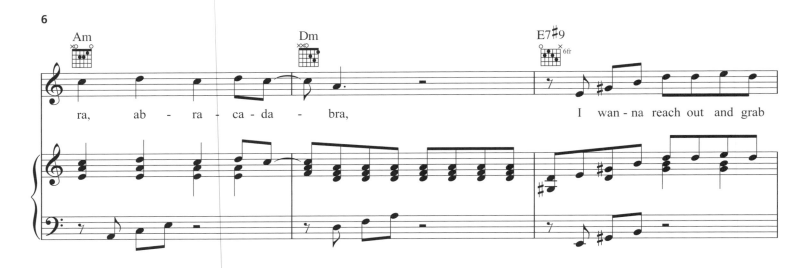

ra, ab - ra - ca - da - bra, I wan - na reach out and grab

ya. Ab - ra, ab - ra - ca - da - bra,

ab - ra - ca - da - bra. You make me hot, you

make me ___ sigh. __ You make me laugh. You make me cry. _____

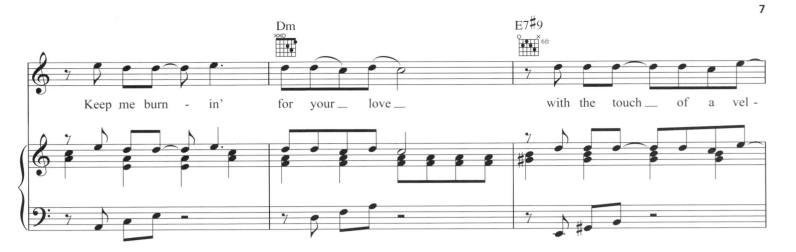

Keep me burn - in' for your __ love __ with the touch __ of a vel -

- vet glove. Ab - ra, ab - ra - ca - da - bra,

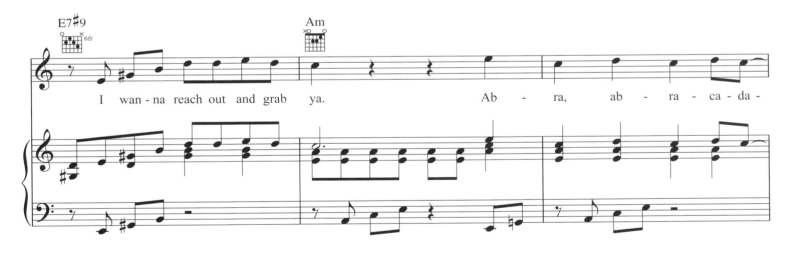

I wan - na reach out and grab ya. Ab - ra, ab - ra - ca - da -

- bra, ab - ra - ca - da - bra.

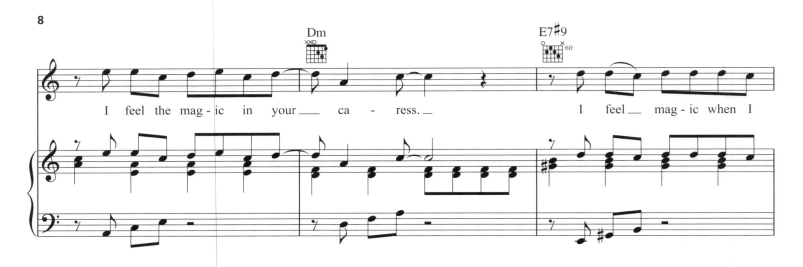

I feel the mag-ic in your ca - ress. I feel mag-ic when I

touch your dress. Silk and sat - in, leath-er and lace.

Black pant-ies with an an-gel's face. I see the mag-ic

in your eyes. I hear the mag-ic in your sighs.

Just when I think I'm gon - na get a - way, __ I hear those words that

you al - ways say. __ Ab - ra, ab - ra - ca - da - bra,

I wan - na reach out and grab ya. Ab - ra, ab - ra - ca - da -

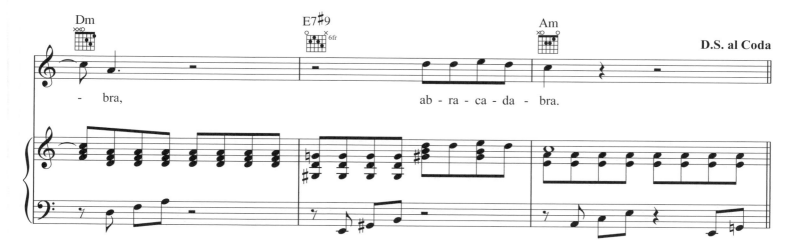

- bra, ab - ra - ca - da - bra.

D.S. al Coda

Kiss me, ba - by, let the fire get high - er, _____ yeah, _____

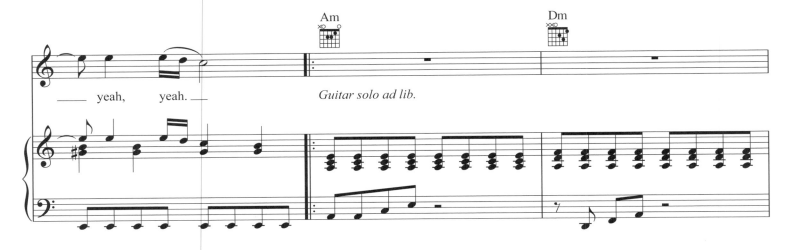

_____ yeah, yeah. _____

Guitar solo ad lib.

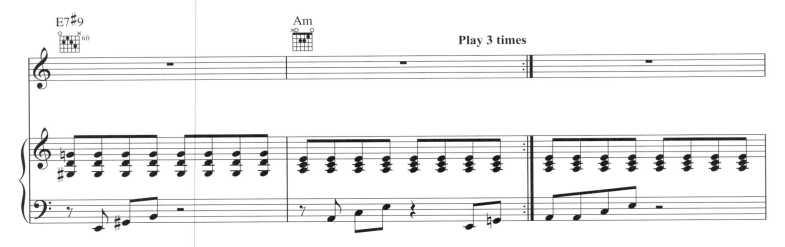

Play 3 times

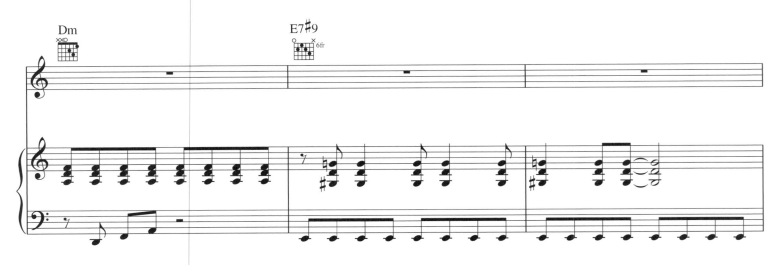

End solo

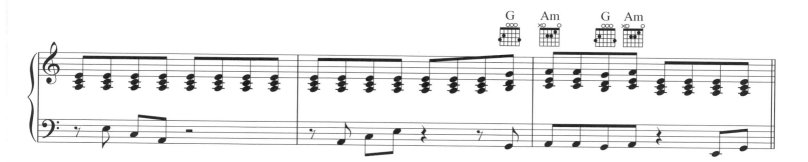

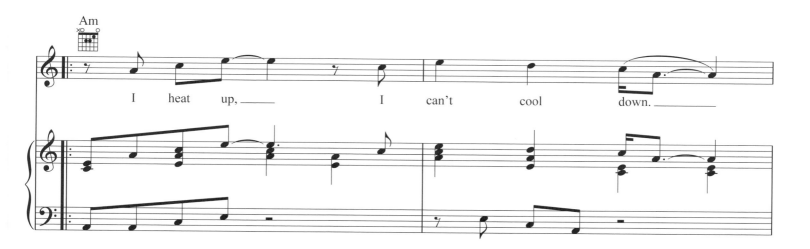

I heat up, ____ I can't cool down. ____

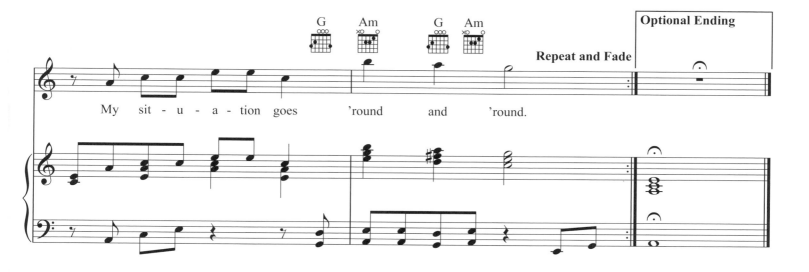

My sit - u - a - tion goes 'round and 'round.

Repeat and Fade

Optional Ending

BAD, BAD LEROY BROWN

Words and Music by
JIM CROCE

Moderate Boogie-Rock tempo

Well, the South -- side of Chi -- ca -- go is the bad --
-- roy he a gam -- bler and he like ___
-- day 'bout a week a -- go, Le --

-- dest part of town, ___ and if you go down there ___ you bet -- ter
___ his fan -- cy clothes, ___ and he like ___ to wave ___ his
-- roy shoot -- in' dice, ___ and at the edge of the bar ___ sat a

just be -- ware ___ of a man name of Le -- roy Brown. ___ Now
dia -- mond rings ___ in front of ev -- 'ry -- bod -- y's nose. ___ He got a
girl name of Dor -- is and, ___ oh, that ___ girl looked nice. ___ Well, ___ he

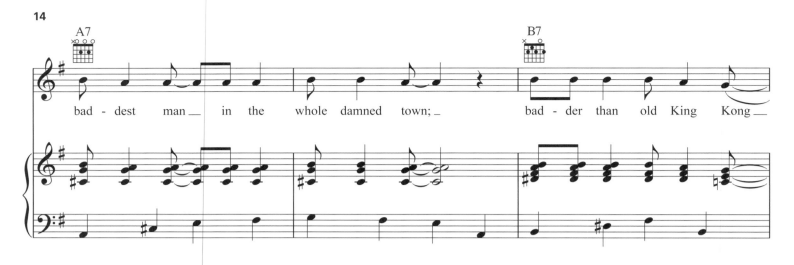

bad-dest man __ in the whole damned town; __ bad-der than old King Kong __

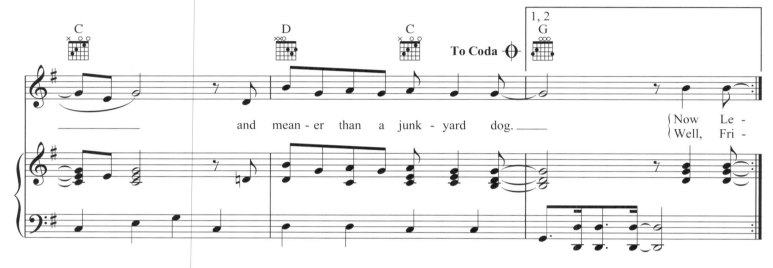

_____ and mean-er than a junk-yard dog. _____ { Now Le- { Well, Fri-

__ Well, the two __ men took to fight-in', and when they

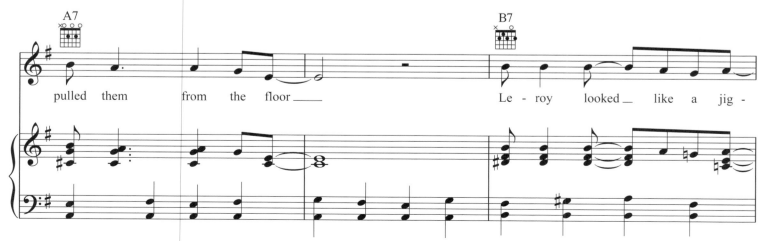

pulled them from the floor _____ Le-roy looked __ like a jig-

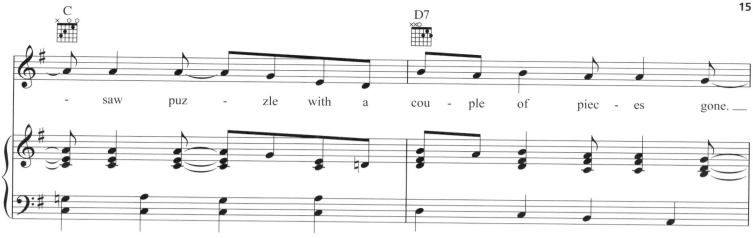

-saw puz - zle with a cou - ple of piec - es gone.___

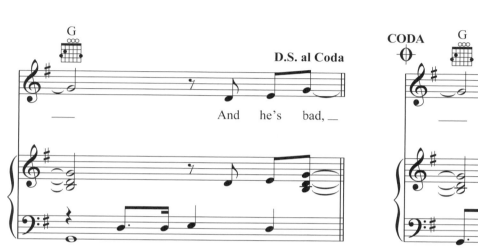

D.S. al Coda

___ And he's bad, ___

CODA

___ Yes, you were

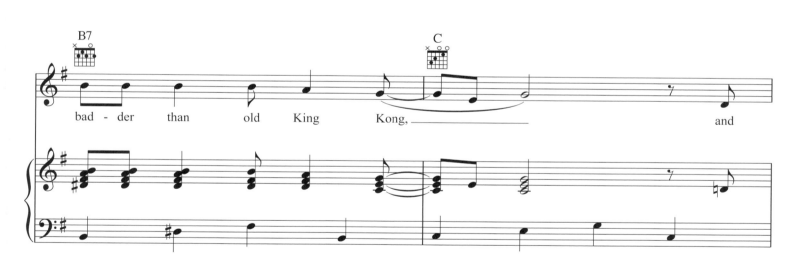

bad - der than old King Kong, _____ and

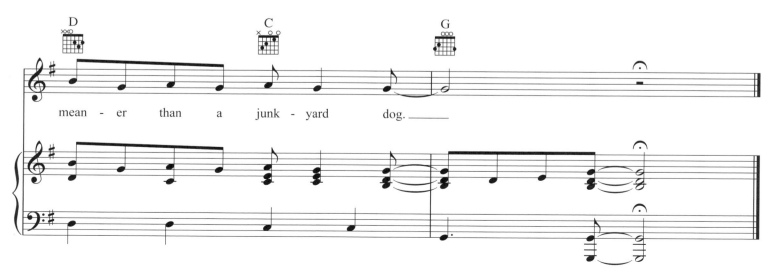

mean - er than a junk - yard dog. _____

BEAT IT

Words and Music by
MICHAEL JACKSON

Moderately fast

They told him, "Don't you ev - er come a - round here. Don't wan - na see your face; you bet - ter
They're out to get you. Bet - ter leave while you can. Don't wan - na be a boy; you wan - na

Instrumental

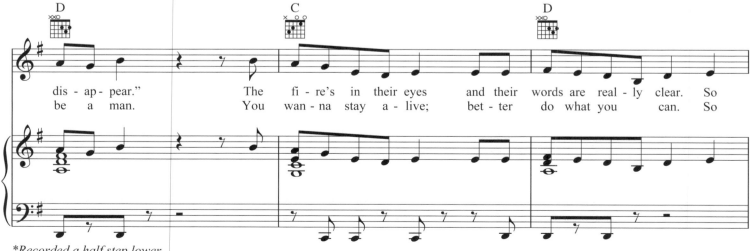

dis - ap - pear." The fi - re's in their eyes and their words are real - ly clear. So
be a man. You wan - na stay a - live; bet - ter do what you can. So

*Recorded a half step lower.

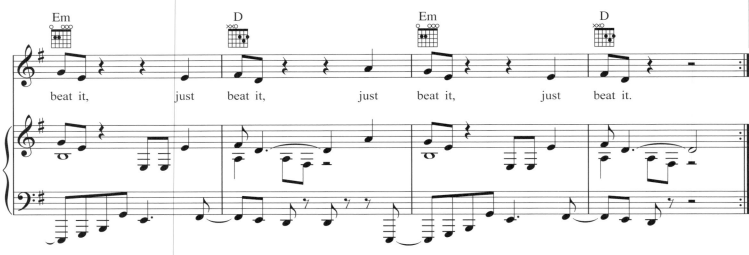

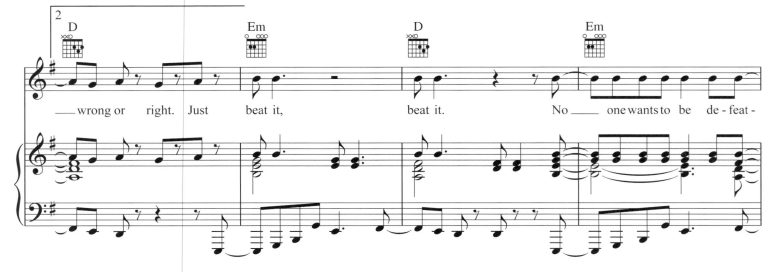

-ed. Show - in' how funk-y, strong __ is your fight. It __

__ does-n't mat-ter who's __ wrong or right. Just beat it. Beat it.

Beat it. Beat it.

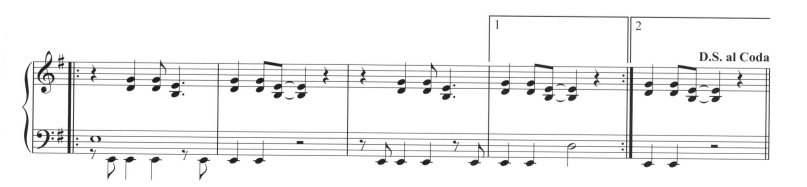

D.S. al Coda

BLUE SUEDE SHOES

Words and Music by
CARL LEE PERKINS

Brightly, not too fast

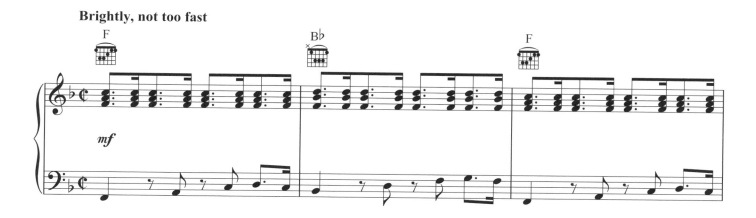

Well, it's one for the mon-ey, two for the show,

three to get read-y, now go, cat, go! But don't you

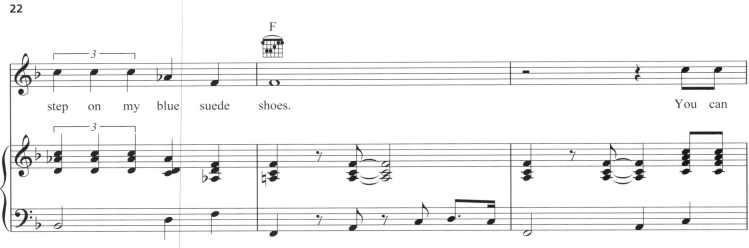

step on my blue suede shoes. You can

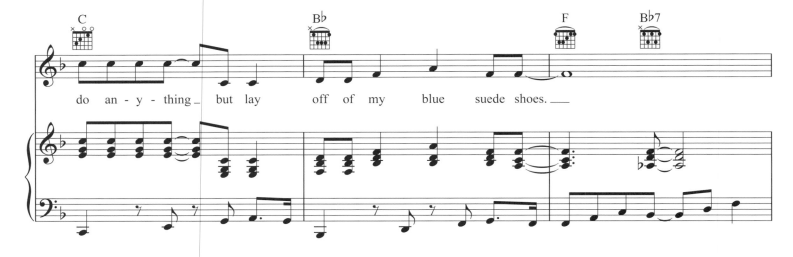

do an-y-thing __ but lay off of my blue suede shoes. ___

Well, you can knock me down, __ step on my face, __
burn my house, __ steal __ my car, __

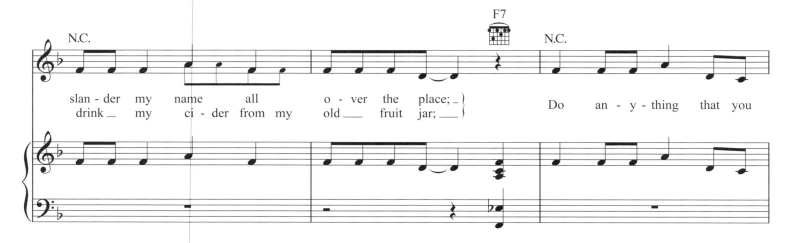

slan-der my name all o-ver the place; __ }
drink __ my ci-der from my old __ fruit jar; ___ } Do an-y-thing that you

want to do, __ but uh-uh, hon-ey, lay off of my shoes. __ Don't you

step on my blue suede shoes. You can

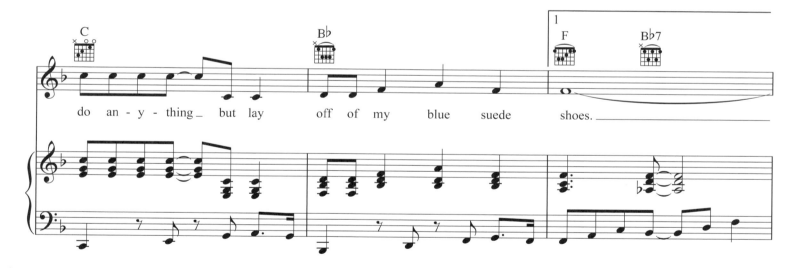

do an-y-thing__ but lay off of my blue suede shoes. __

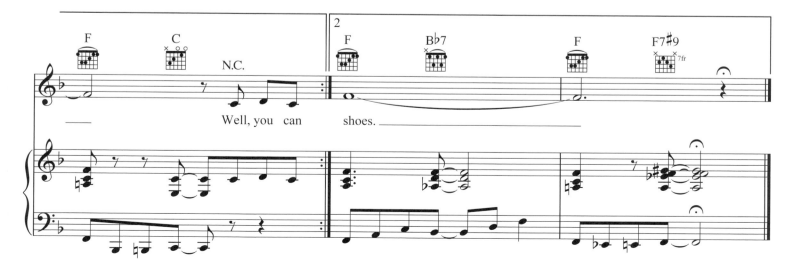

Well, you can shoes. __

BRASS IN POCKET

Words and Music by CHRISSIE HYNDE
and JAMES HONEYMAN-SCOTT

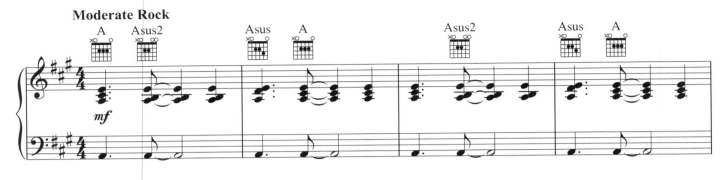

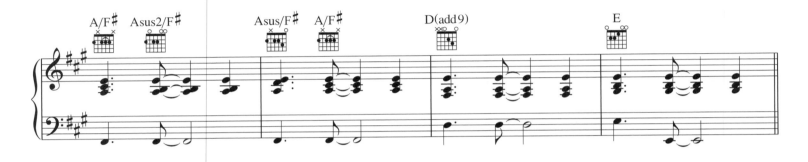

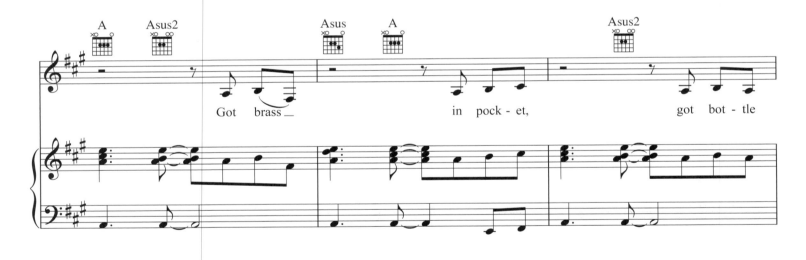

Got brass ___ in pock - et, got bot - tle

I'm ___ gon - na use ___ it. In - ten - tion, I feel in - ven - tive, ___

gon-na make you, make you, make you no - tice. _____ Got mo - tion,
Got rhy - thm,

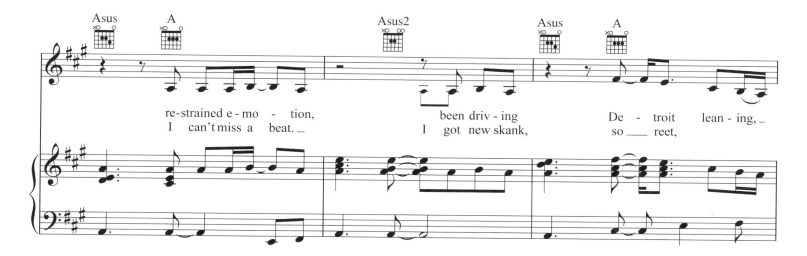

re-strained e - mo - tion,   been driv - ing   De - troit lean - ing, __
I can't miss a beat. __   I got new skank,   so ___ reet,

no rea - son _____   it seems so pleas - ing. _____ }
got some - thing _____   I'm wink - ing at you. _____ }   Gon-na make you, make

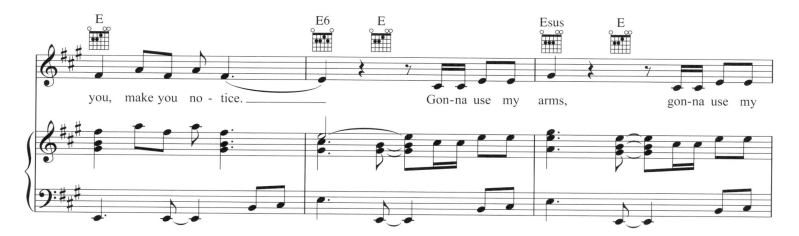

you, make you no - tice. _____   Gon-na use my arms,   gon-na use my

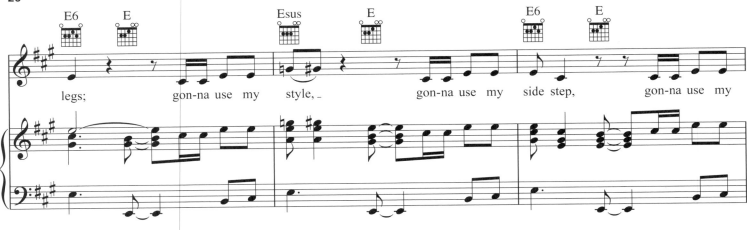

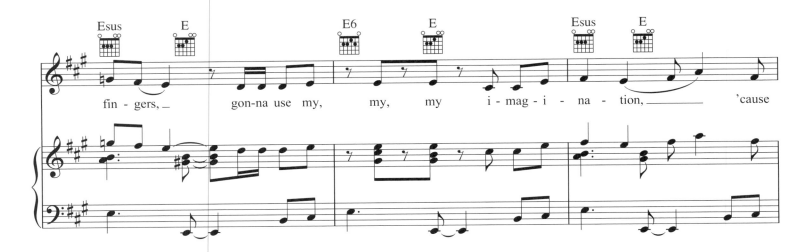

have some of your ___ at - ten - tion, ___ give it to me.   ten - tion, ___ give it to me, ___ 'cause ___

ten - tion, ___   give it to me. ___

Oh oh   oh, _____

and when you   walk. ___

CALIFORNIA GIRLS

Words and Music by BRIAN WILSON
and MIKE LOVE

Well,

East Coast girls are hip,___ I real - ly dig ___ those styles they wear;
West Coast girls has the sun - shine, and ___ the girls ___ all get so tanned;

*Recorded one half step higher.

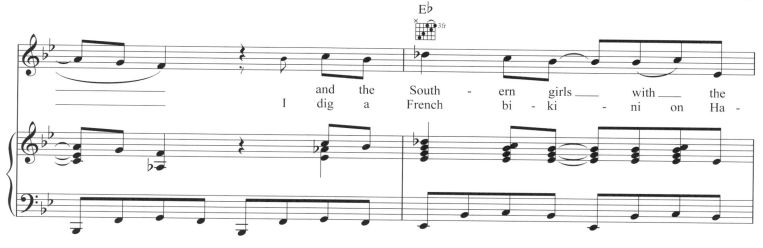

and the South - ern girls ___ with ___ the
I dig a French bi - ki - ni on Ha -

way they talk ___ they knock me out when I'm down there. ___ The
wai - ian is - land dolls by a palm tree in the sand. ___ I've

Mid - west farm - er's daugh - ters real - ly make you feel al - right.
been all a - round this great ___ big world, ___ and I've seen all kinds of girls. ___

And the North - ern girls ___ with ___ the
Yeah, but I could - n't wait to get

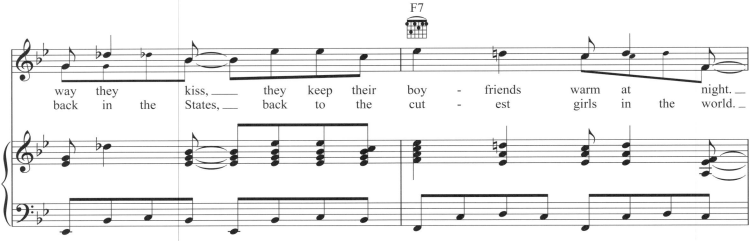

way they the kiss, ___ they keep their boy - friends warm at the night. ___
back in the States, ___ back to the cut - est girls in the world. ___

___ I wish they all could be ___ Cal - i - for - nia, I

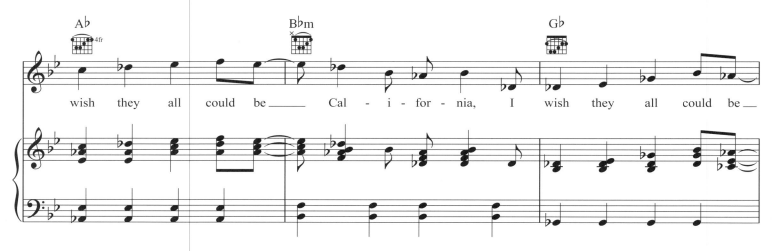

wish they all could be ___ Cal - i - for - nia, I wish they all could be ___

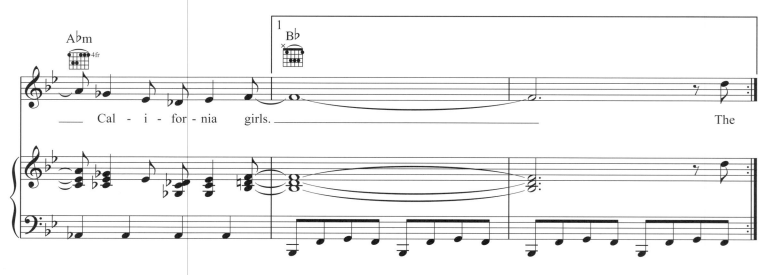

___ Cal - i - for - nia girls. ___ The

I wish they all could be _____ Cal - i - for - nia, I

Repeat and Fade

wish they all could be _____ Cal - i - for - nia, I

Optional Ending

_____ Cal - i - for - nia _____ girls. _____

CALL ME

from the Paramount Motion Picture AMERICAN GIGOLO

Words by DEBORAH HARRY
Music by GIORGIO MORODER

Col-or me your col-or, ba-by, col-or me your car. Col-or me your col-or, dar-ling, I know who you are.

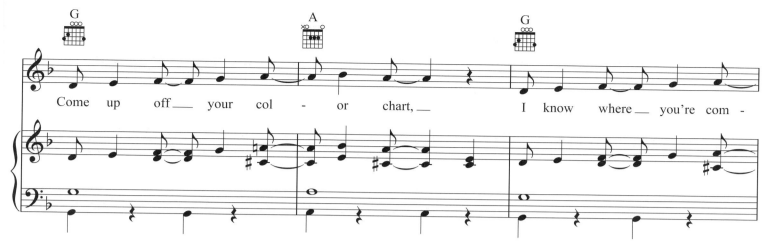

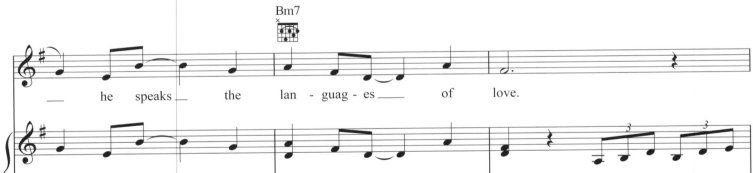

chia - ma mi.   Oo, _____ ap - pelle __ moi,

mon che - rie, _____ ap - pelle moi,   an - y - time, _____

_____ an - y - place, _____ an - y - where, __ an - y - way, _____

an - y - time, _____

an - y - place, _____ an - y - where, _____ an - y day. _____

Call me, _____

in my life call me,

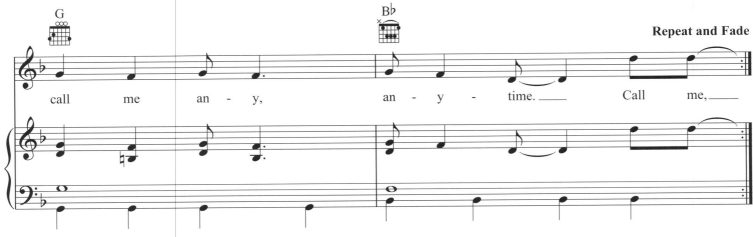

Repeat and Fade

call me an - y, an - y - time. _____ Call me, _____

CROCODILE ROCK

Words and Music by ELTON JOHN
and BERNIE TAUPIN

Light-hearted Rock

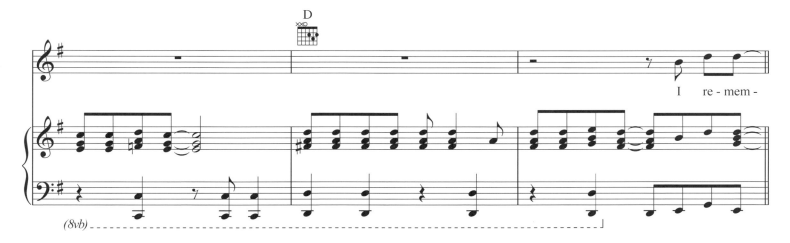

I re-mem-

(1., 3.) -ber when rock was young. _____ Me and Su - sie had so much fun _____
(2.) _____ went by _____ and rock just died. _____ Su - sie went and left me for some

croc - o - dile rock. Well,
rock __ would last. Well, } croc-o-dile rock - in' is some-thing shock - in' when your

feet just can't keep still. __ I nev - er knew me a

bet - ter time __ and I guess __ I nev - er __ will. __ Oh, __

__ Lawd - y, ma - ma, those Fri - day nights __ when Su - sie wore __ her

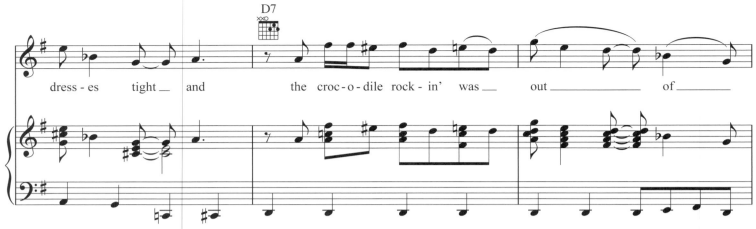

dress - es tight ____ and   the croc - o - dile rock - in' was ____ out _____ of _____

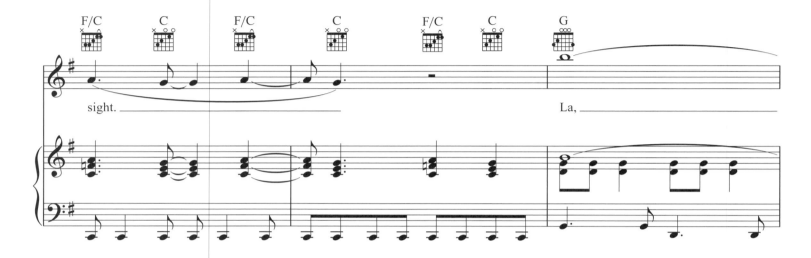

sight. _____   La, _____

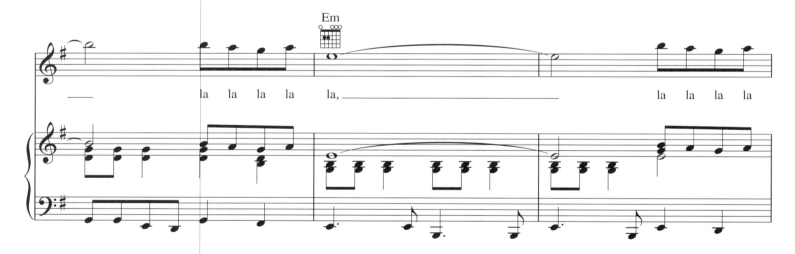

____ la la la la la, _____   la la la la

la, _____   la la la la la.

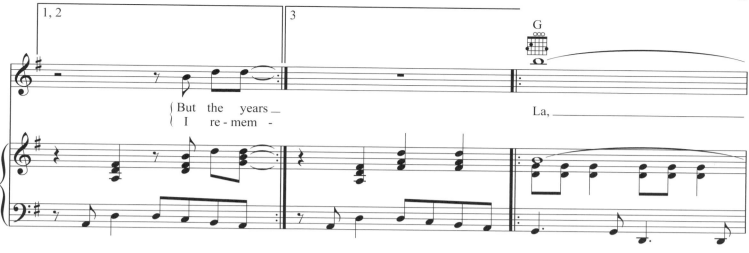

But the years —
I re-mem -

La,

la la la la la, —

la la la la

la, —

la la la la la.

Repeat and Fade

Optional Ending

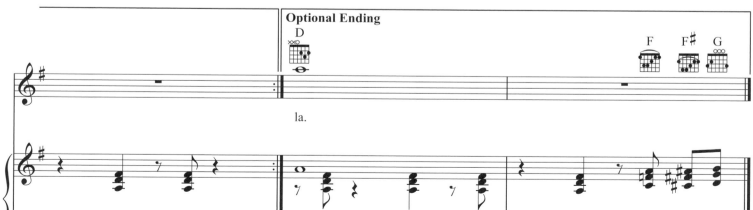

la.

CLOCKS

Words and Music by GUY BERRYMAN, JON BUCKLAND,
WILL CHAMPION and CHRIS MARTIN

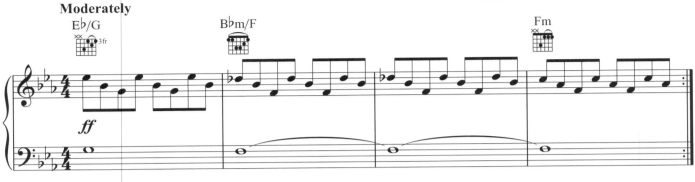

Lights go out and I can't be saved. ___ Tides that I tried to
Con - fu - sion ___ nev - er stops. ___ Clos - ing ___ walls and

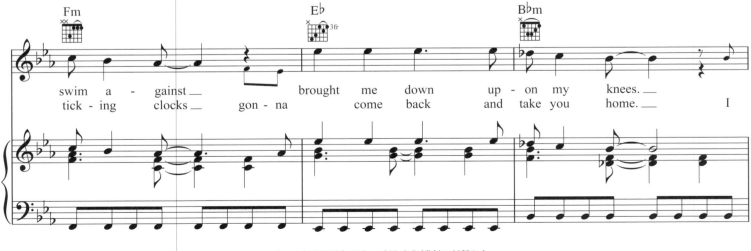

swim a - gainst ___ brought me down up - on my knees. ___
tick - ing clocks ___ gon - na come down back and take you home. ___ I

Oh, I beg, I beg and plead. _ Sing - in', come out of
could not stop that you now know. _ Sing - in', come out up-

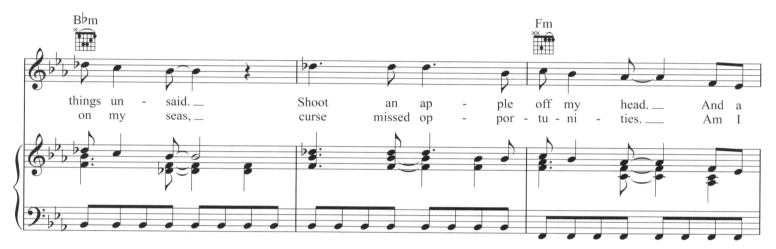

things un - said. _ Shoot an ap - ple off my head. _ And a
on my seas, _ curse an missed op - por - tu - ni - ties. _ Am I

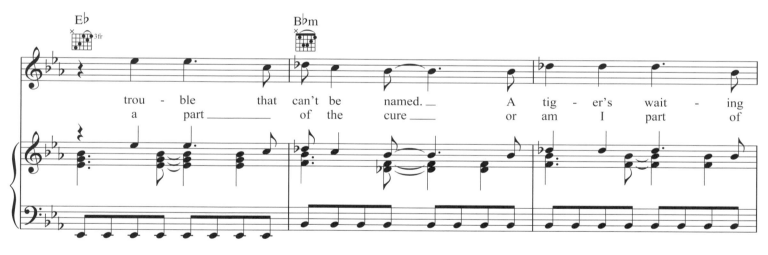

trou - ble that can't be named. _ A tig - er's wait - ing
a part _ of the cure _ or am I part of

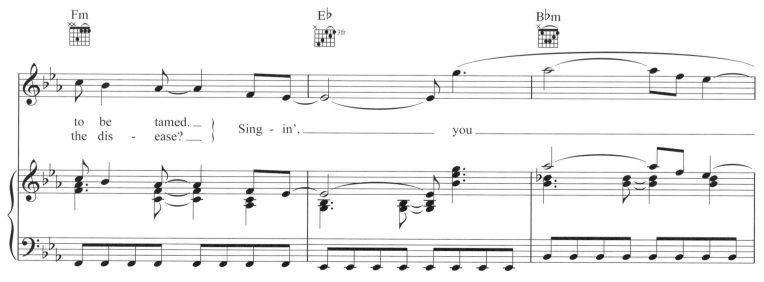

to be tamed. _ } Sing - in', _____ you _____
the dis - ease? _ }

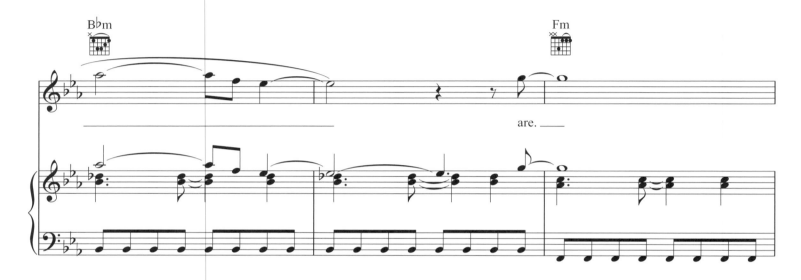

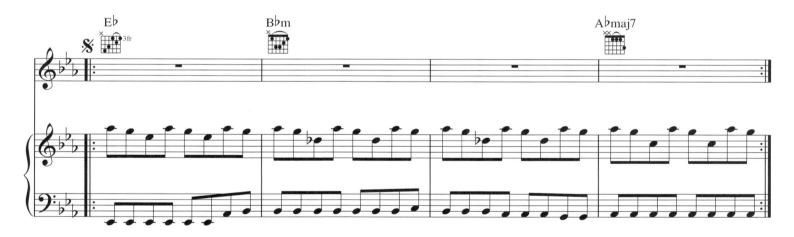

And noth - ing else com - pares. ____

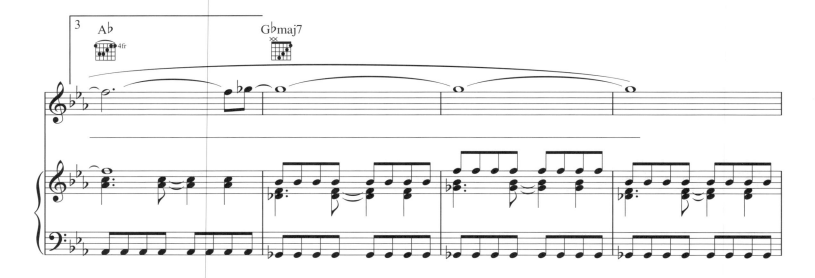

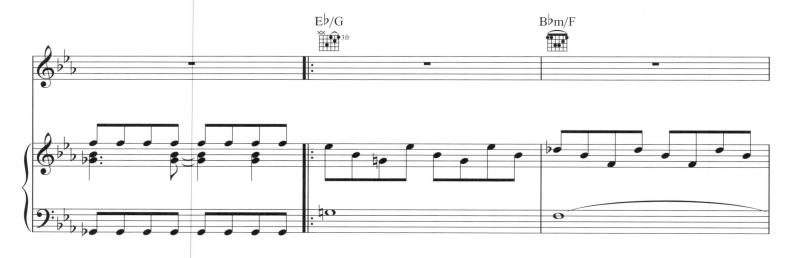

D.S. al Coda
(with repeats)

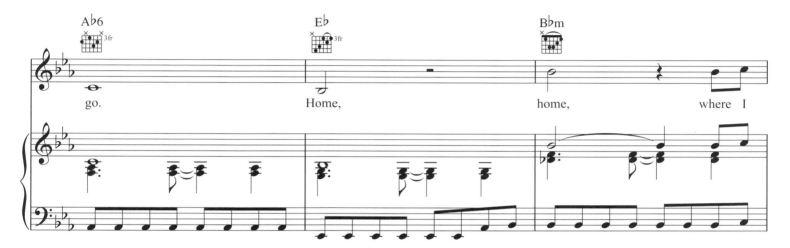

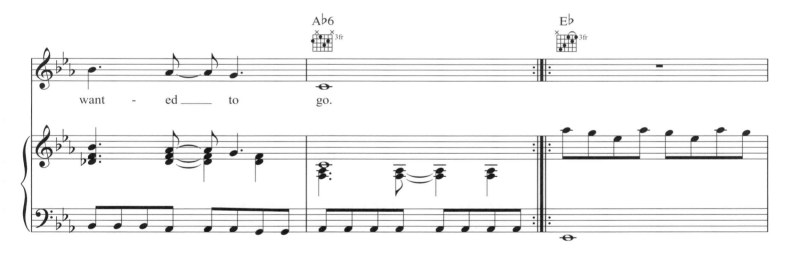

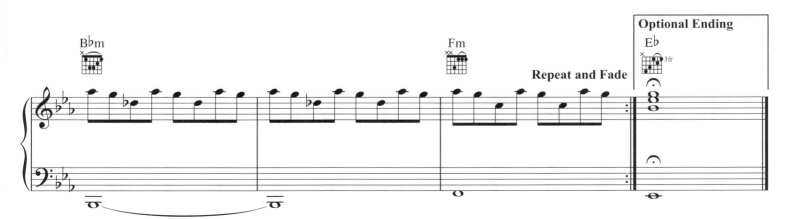

DON'T YOU WANT ME

Words and Music by PHIL OAKEY,
ADRIAN WRIGHT and JO CALLIS

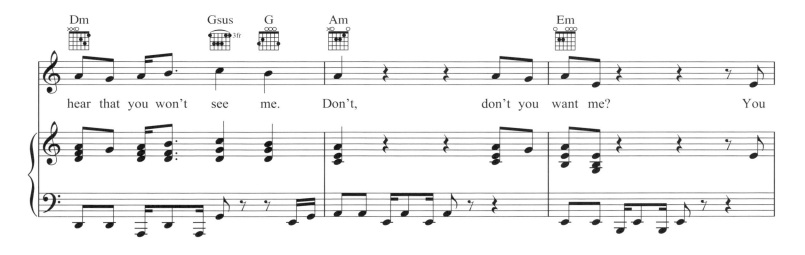

much too late __ to find when you think you've changed your mind. __ You'd

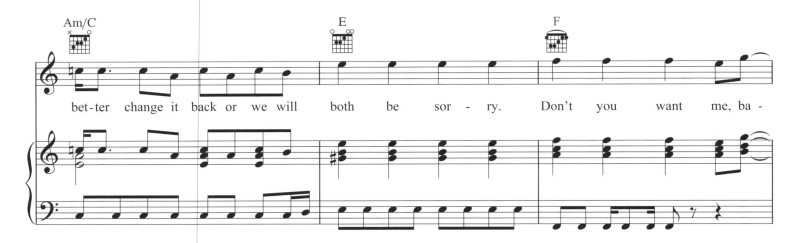

bet-ter change it back or we will both be sor - ry. Don't you want me, ba -

- by? Don't you want me, oh? _____

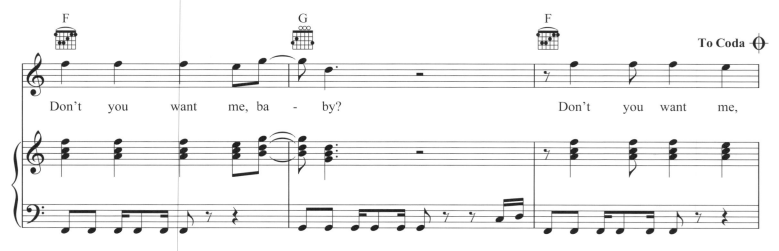

Don't you want me, ba - by? Don't you want me,

To Coda ⊕

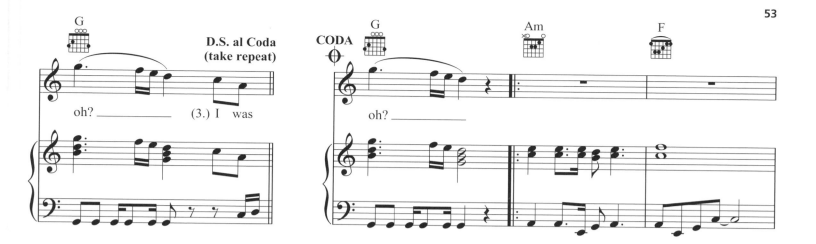

Additional Lyrics

3. I was working as a waitress in a cocktail bar,
   That much is true.
   But even then I knew I'd find a much better place
   Either with or without you.

4. The five years we had have been such good times,
   I still love you.
   But now I think it's time I live my life on my own.
   I guess it's just what I must do.

EVERY BREATH YOU TAKE

Music and Lyrics by
STING

Moderate Rock

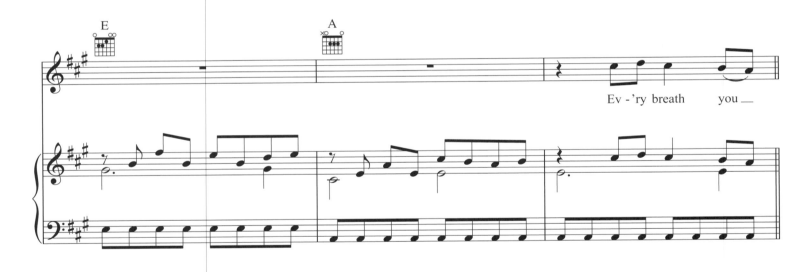

Ev - 'ry breath you ___

take, ev - 'ry move you ___ make,

ev-'ry bond _ you break, ev-'ry step _ you take, I'll be watch-ing you.

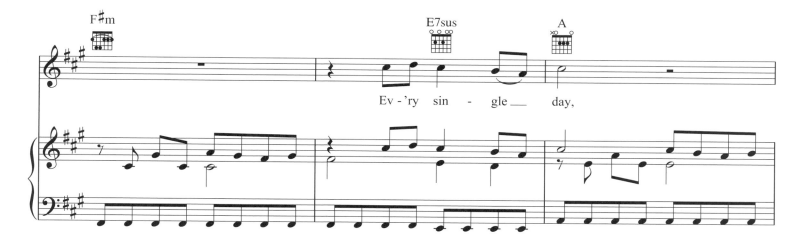

Ev-'ry sin - gle _ day,

ev-'ry word you _ say, ev-'ry game _ you play,

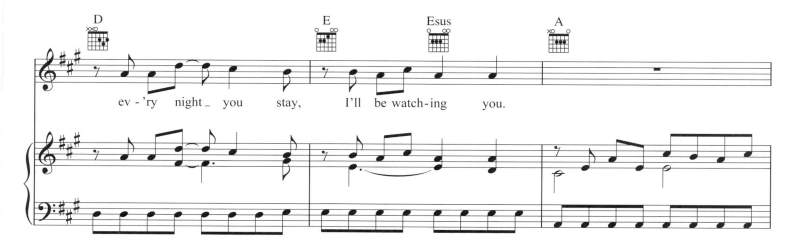

ev-'ry night _ you stay, I'll be watch-ing you.

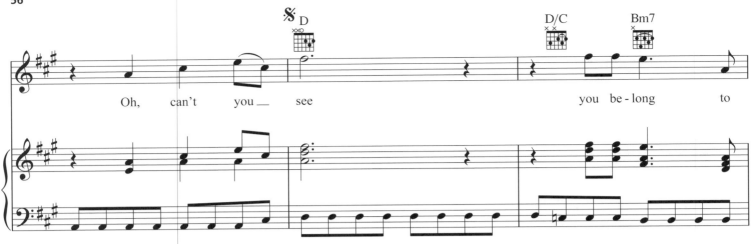

Oh, can't you __ see you be-long to

me? How my poor heart _____ aches __

with ev-'ry step __ you take. Ev-'ry move you __

make, ev-'ry vow you __ break,

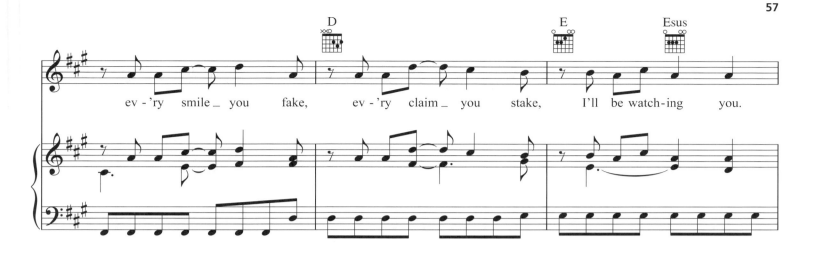

ev-'ry smile _ you fake, ev-'ry claim _ you stake, I'll be watch-ing you.

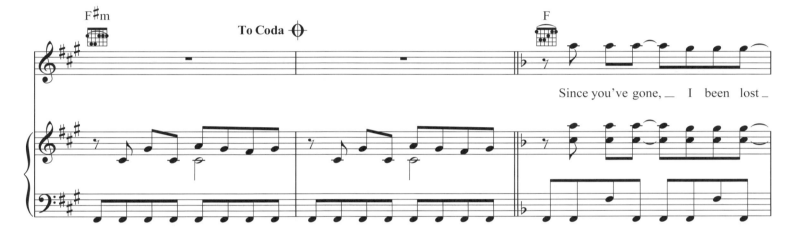

Since you've gone, _ I been lost _

_ with - out _____ a trace, I dream at night I can on - ly see _ your face.

I look a - round, but it's you I can't _ re - place. I feel so cold and I

long for your _ em- brace. I keep cry - ing, ba - by, ba - by, please. _

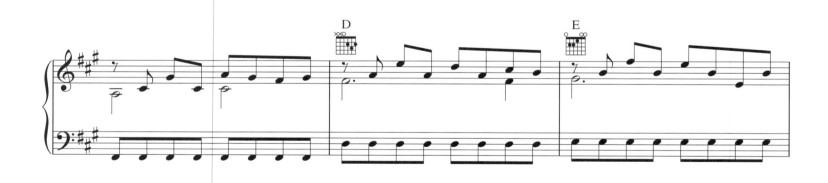

Oh, can't you ____

Ev - 'ry move ____ you make, ev - 'ry step ____ you take,

I'll be watch-ing you.

I'll be watch - ing

you. (Ev-'ry breath __ you take, ev-'ry move __ you make, ev-'ry bond __ you break,
you. (Ev-'ry move __ you make, ev-'ry vow __ you break, ev-'ry smile __ you fake,

ev-'ry step ___ you take, } ev-'ry sin - gle day,
ev-'ry claim ___ you stake, }
I'll be watch - ing you.

Repeat and Fade

ev-'ry word __ you say, ev-'ry game __ you play, ev-'ry night __ you stay.)
I'll be watch-ing

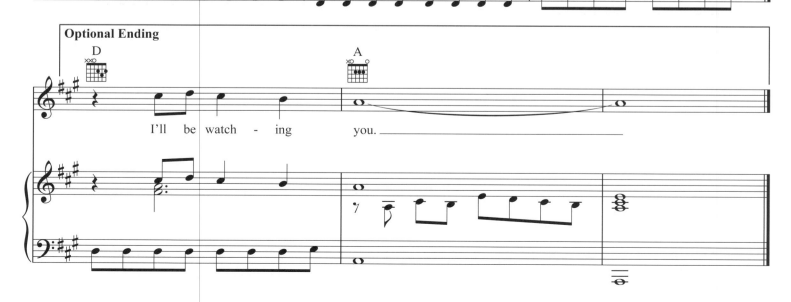

Optional Ending

I'll be watch - ing you. ___

FAME

Words and Music by JOHN LENNON,
DAVID BOWIE and CARLOS ALOMAR

Solid Rock beat

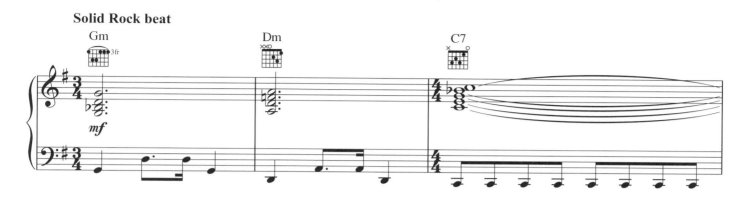

Fame _____ makes a man _____ take things o - ver. _____ Fame _____ lets him

Fame, _____ what you like ___ is in the lim- o. _____ Fame, _____ what you

loose, hard to swal - low. _____ Fame _____ puts you there ___ where things are hol - low, _____

get is no to - mor - row. _____ Fame, _____ what you need ___ you have to bor - row, _____

FREE FALLIN'

Words and Music by TOM PETTY
and JEFF LYNNE

Moderate Rock

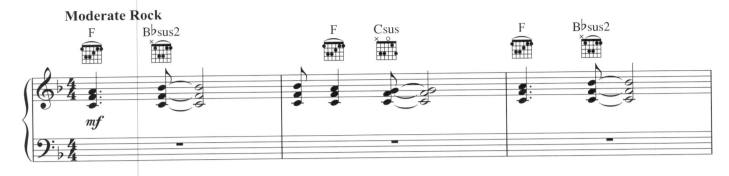

She's a good girl; ___ loves her ma - ma, loves

Je - sus ___ and A - mer - i - ca, too. ___ She's a good girl; ___

cra - zy 'bout ___ El - vis, loves hors - es ___ and her boy - friend, too. ___

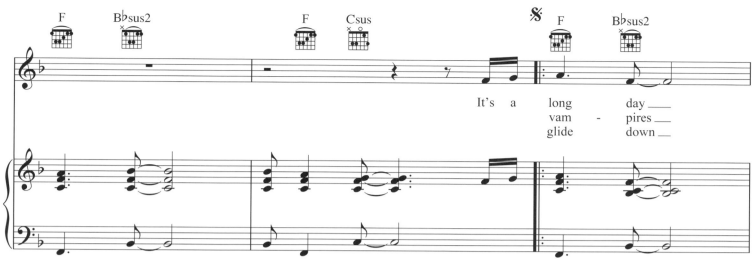

It's a long day _____
vam - pires _____
glide down _____

liv - in' in Re - se - da. There's a free - way _____ run - nin' through the yard. _____ And I'm a
walk-in' through the val - ley move _____ west down _____ Ven-tur - a Boul - e - vard. _____ And all the
o - ver Mul - hol - land. I wan - na write her _____ name in the sky. _____ I wan - na

bad boy _____ 'cause I don't e - ven miss _____ her. I'm a bad boy _____ for
bad boys _____ are stand - ing in the shad - ows. And the good girls _____ are
free fall _____ out in - to noth - in'. Gon - na leave this _____

break-in' her __ heart. __
home with bro-ken hearts. __
world for a while. __
And I'm free, free

fall - in'. Yeah, I'm free,

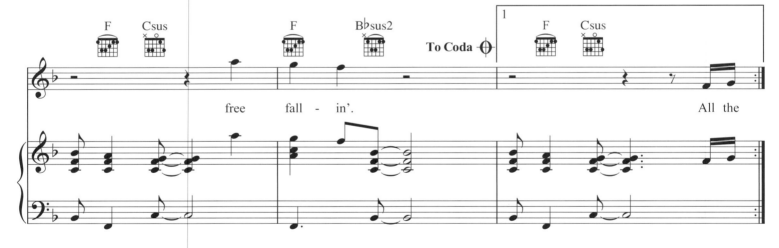

free fall - in'. All the

To Coda ⊕

Instrumental solo

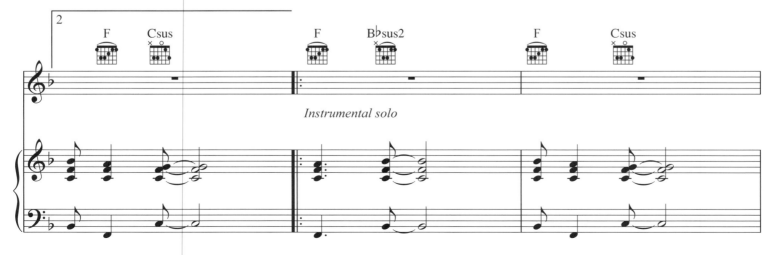

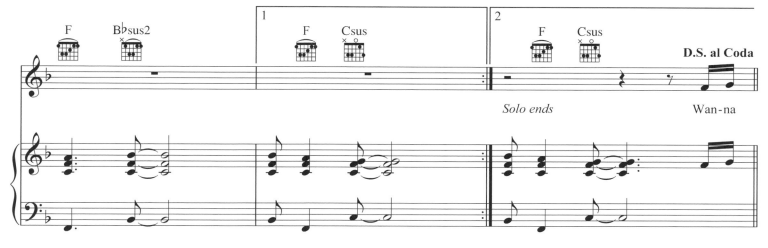

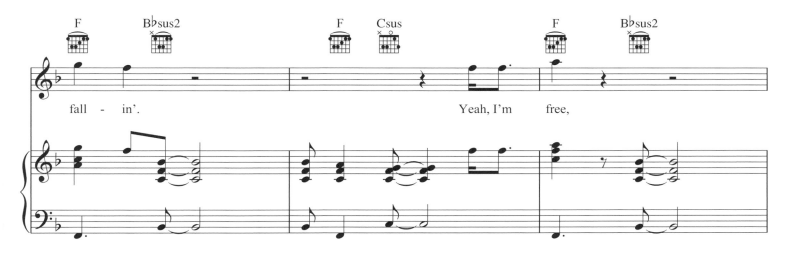

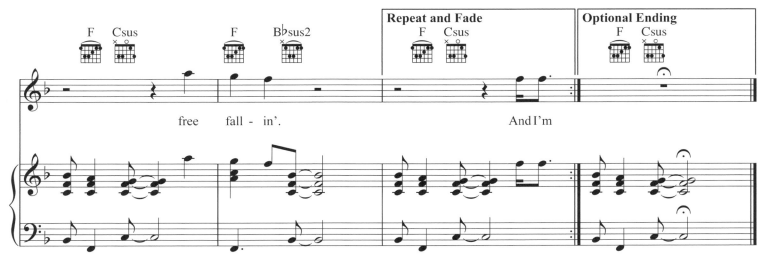

HEY, SOUL SISTER

Words and Music by PAT MONAHAN,
ESPEN LIND and AMUND BJORKLAND

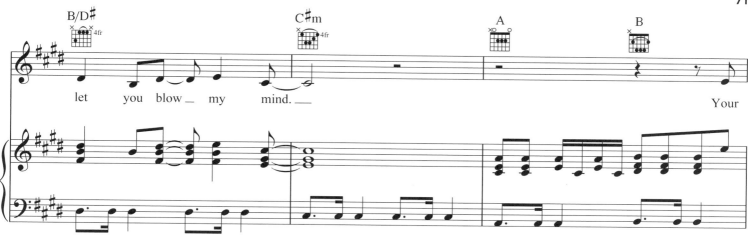

let you blow — my mind. —   Your

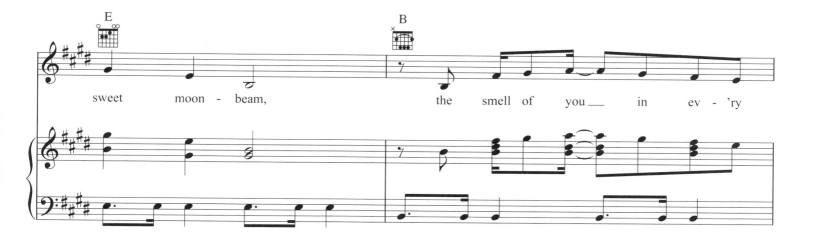

sweet moon - beam,   the smell of you — in ev - 'ry

sin - gle dream I — dream, —   I knew when we col - lid -

- ed you're the one — I have de - cid - ed   who's one of my — kind. —

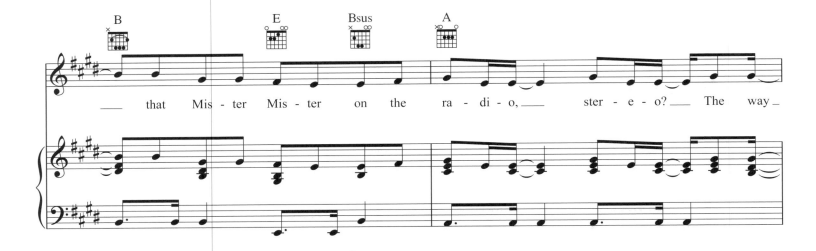

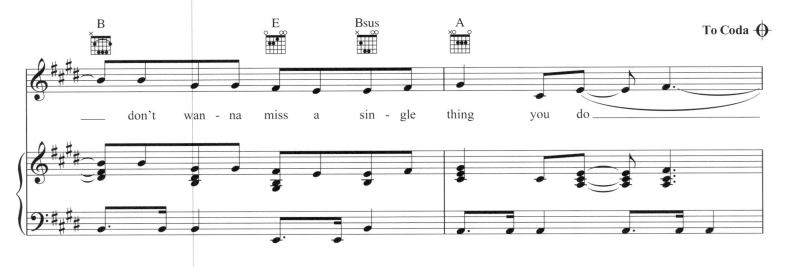

to - night. _____ Hey, _____ hey, _____

_____ hey! _____

Just in time, _____ I'm so glad you have a

one - track mind like _____ me. _____ You gave my life di - rec -

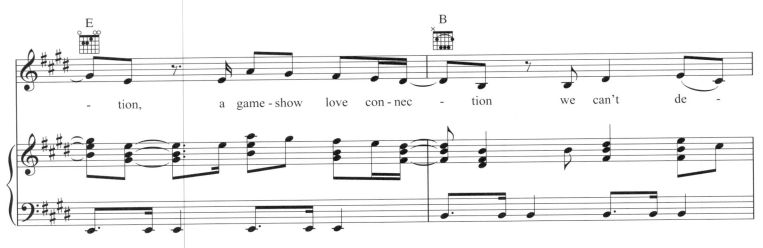

-tion, a game-show love con-nec - tion we can't de-

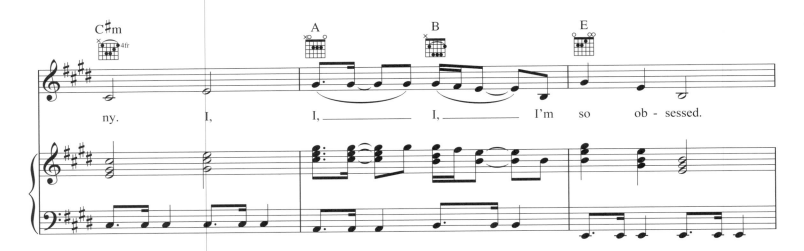

ny. I, I, _____ I, _____ I'm so ob-sessed.

My heart is bound to beat right out my un-trimmed _ chest. _

I be-lieve _ in you. _ Like a vir - gin, you're Ma-don-

- na, and I'm al - ways gon - na wan - na blow_ your mind. _____

D.S. al Coda

CODA

to - night. _ The way you can cut a rug, _

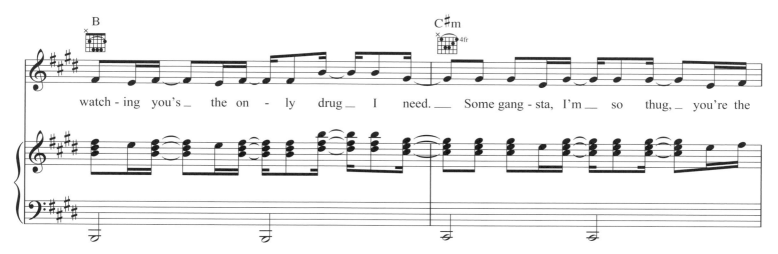

watch - ing you's_ the on - ly drug_ I need. _ Some gang - sta, I'm _ so thug, _ you're the

on - ly one _ I'm dream - ing of. _ You see, _ I can be my - self _ now fi - nal - ly. _

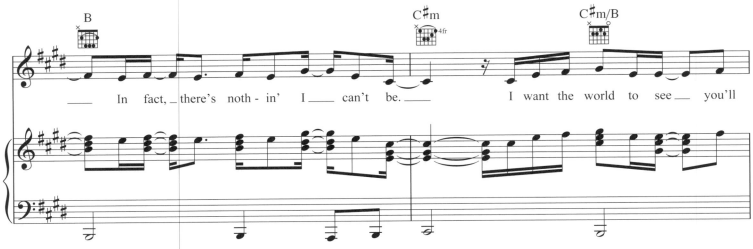

In fact, there's noth-in' I ___ can't be. ___ I want the world to see ___ you'll

be ___ with ___ me. Hey, soul sis-ter, ain't ___ that Mis-ter Mis-ter on the

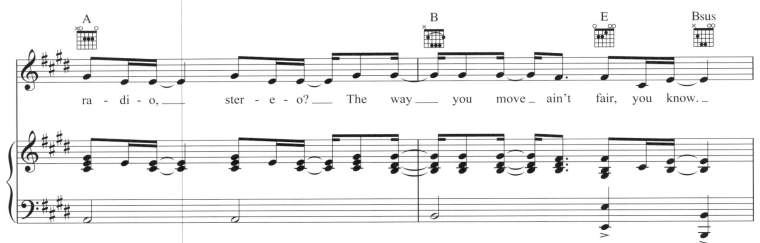

ra-di-o, ___ ster-e-o? ___ The way ___ you move ___ ain't fair, you know. ___

Hey, soul sis-ter, I ___ don't wan-na miss a sin-gle thing you do ___ to-night. ___

Hey, soul sis - ter, I

don't wan - na miss a sin - gle thing you do to - night.

Hey, hey, hey,

to - night. to - night.

HOTEL CALIFORNIA

Words and Music by DON HENLEY,
GLENN FREY and DON FELDER

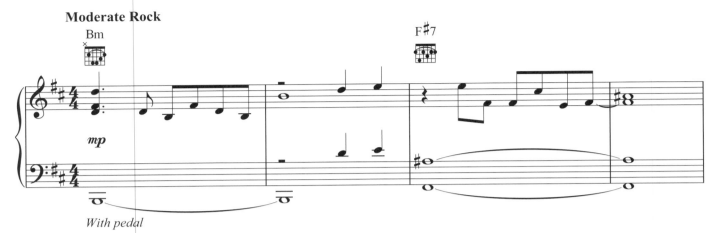

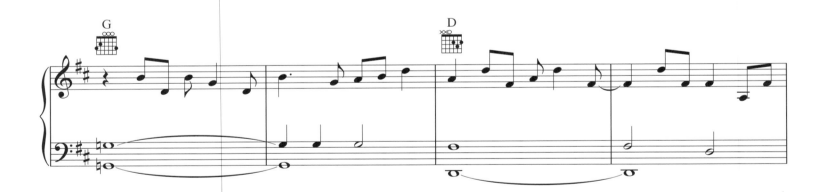

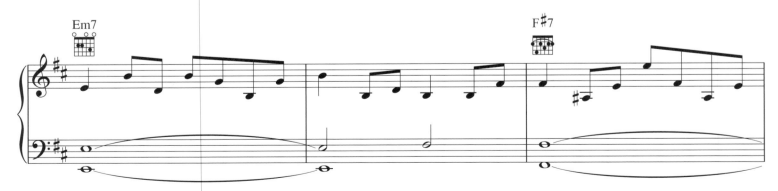

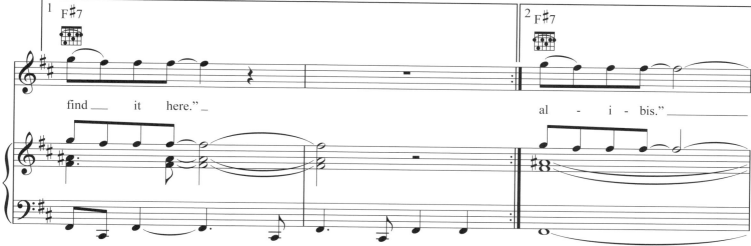

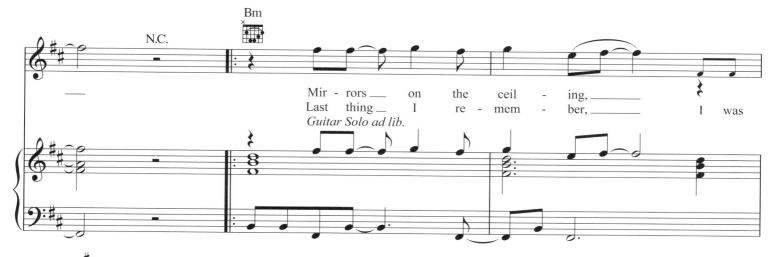

IF YOU LOVE SOMEBODY SET THEM FREE

Music and Lyrics by
STING

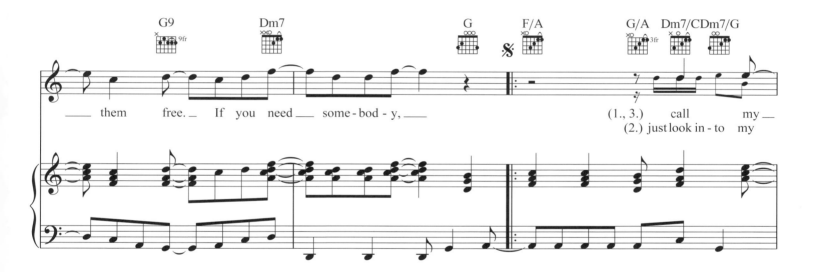

if you love ___ some-one, if you love _

___ some-bod - y, if you love ___ some-

one, set them free. (Free, free, set ___ them free.) Set them

free. (Free, free, set ___ them free.) Set them free. (Free, free, set _

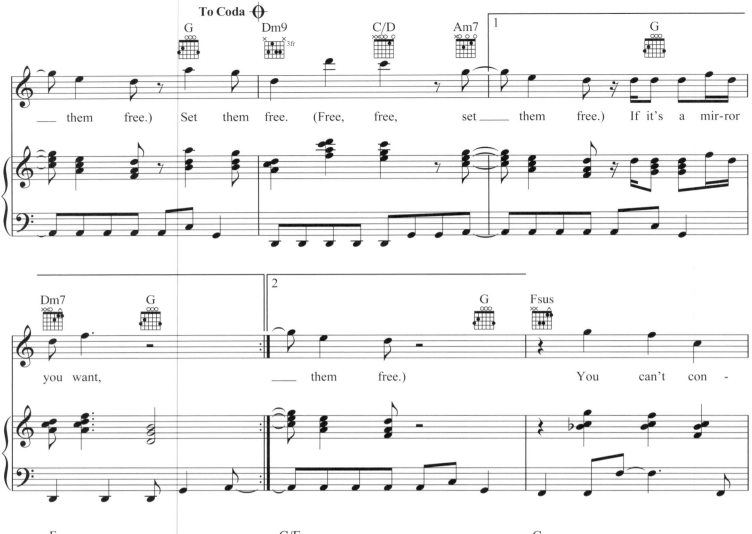

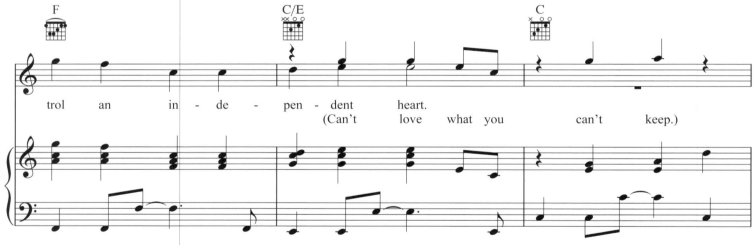

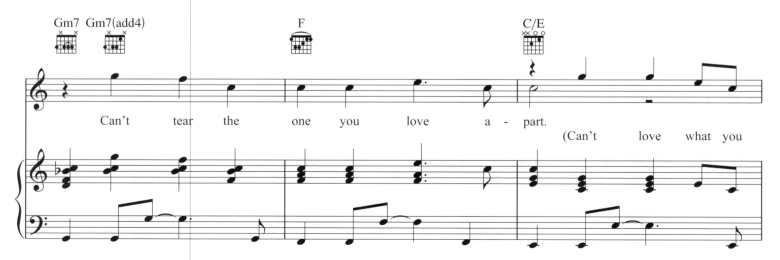

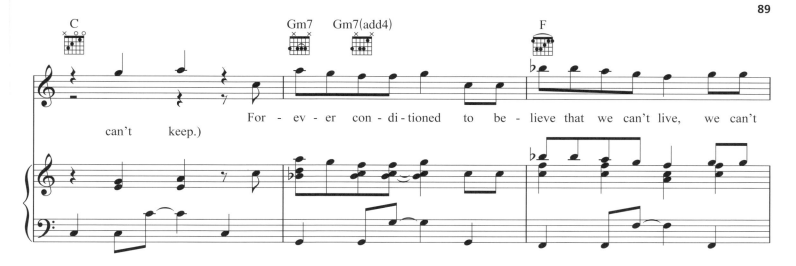

For - ev - er con - di - tioned to be - lieve that we can't live, we can't
can't keep.)

live here and be hap - py with less. ___ With so man - y rich - es, so ___

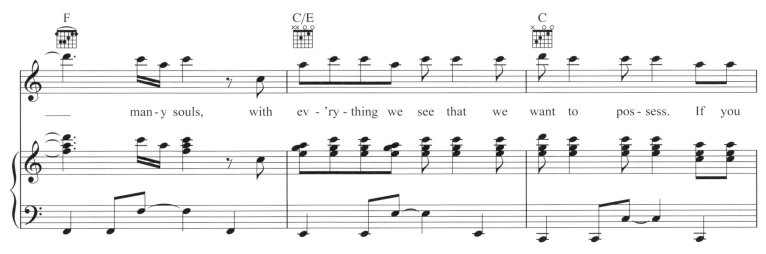

___ man - y souls, with ev - 'ry - thing we see that we want to pos - sess. If you

D.S. al Coda

need some - bod - y, ___

Repeat and Fade

free. (Free, free, set ___ them free.) Set them
Vocal ad lib.

I WANT TO HOLD YOUR HAND

Words and Music by JOHN LENNON
and PAUL McCARTNEY

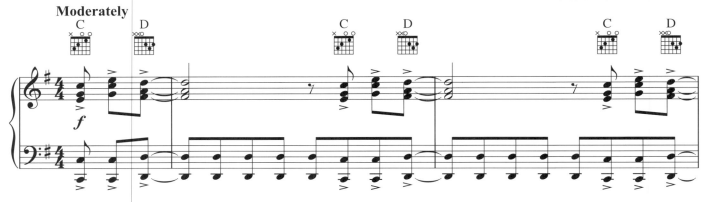

Oh yeah,

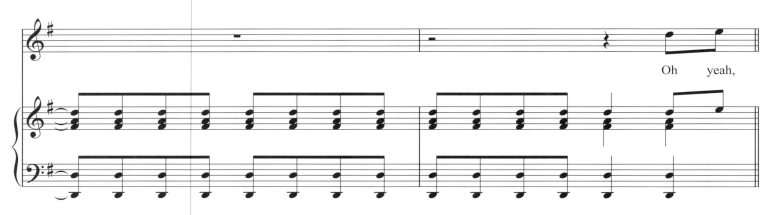

I'll _____ tell you some - thing   I think you'll un - der -
please _____ say to me _____   you'll let me be your

stand.   When I _____ say that some - thing,
man,   and please _____ say to me _____

I want to hold your hand, ___
you'll let me hold your hand. ___
I want to hold your

hand, _____
hand, _____
I want to hold your hand.   Oh, ___
I want to hold your

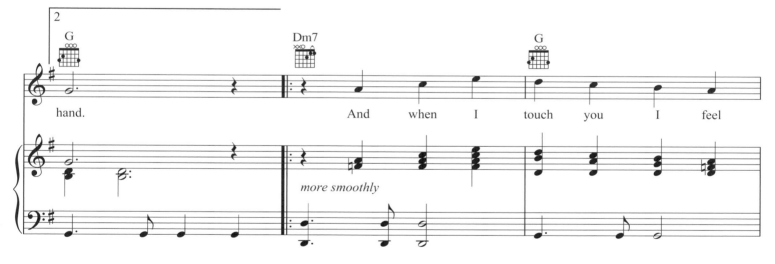

hand.   And when I touch you I feel

more smoothly

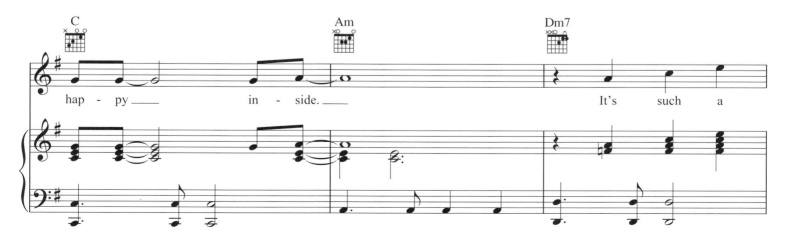

hap-py ___ in - side. ___   It's such a

feel - ing that my love I can't hide, ___ I can't hide, ___

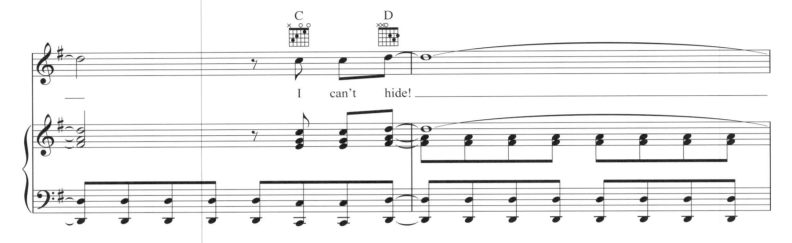

I can't hide! _____

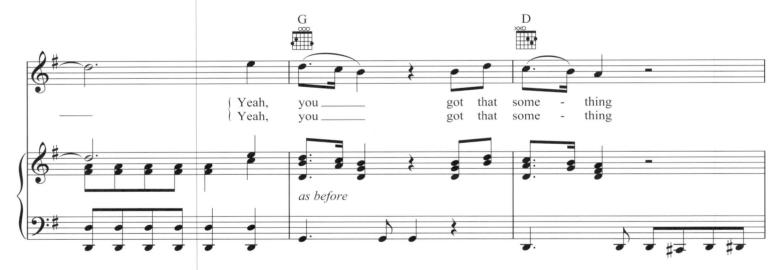

{ Yeah, you _____ got that some - thing
{ Yeah, you _____ got that some - thing

as before

I think you'll un - der - stand. When I _____ say that
I think you'll un - der - stand. When I _____ feel that

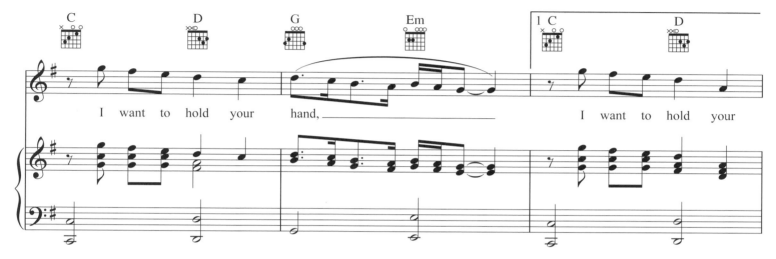

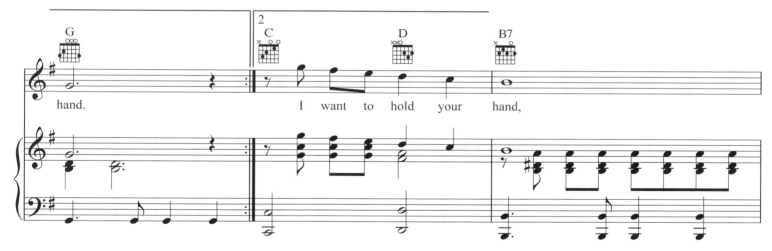

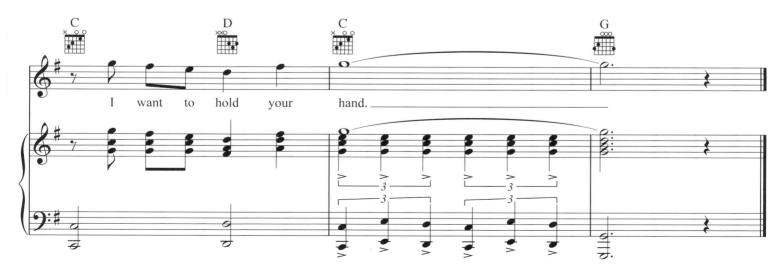

I WANT YOU TO WANT ME

Words and Music by
RICK NIELSEN

Bright Two-beat

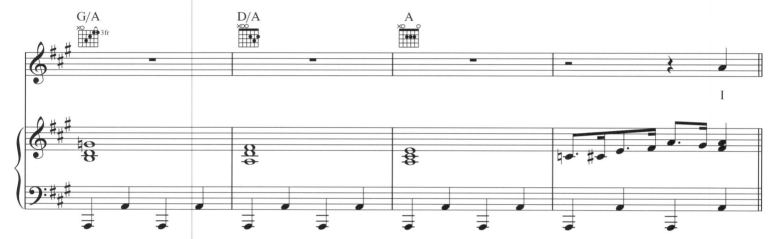

I want you to want ___ me. I

need you to need ___ me. I'd

love you to love ___ me. I'm

To Coda ⊕

beg - gin' you to { beg me.
                { beg me. I'll I

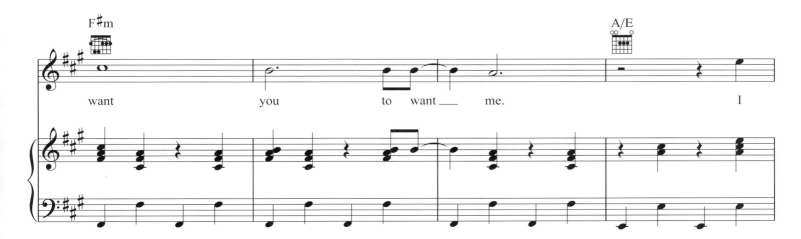

want you to want ___ me. I

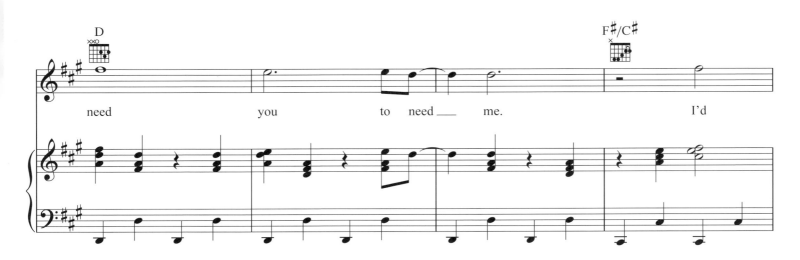

need you to need ___ me. I'd

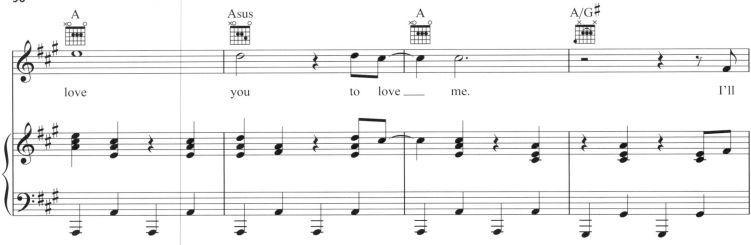

love you to love ___ me. I'll

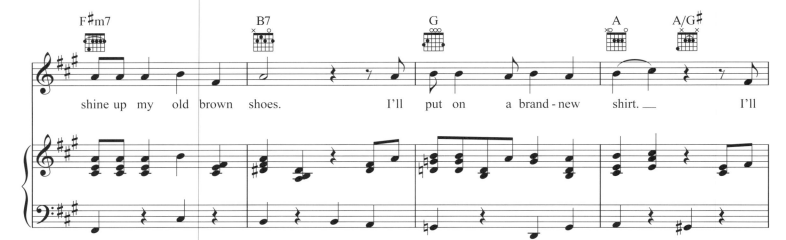

shine up my old brown shoes. I'll put on a brand-new shirt. ___ I'll

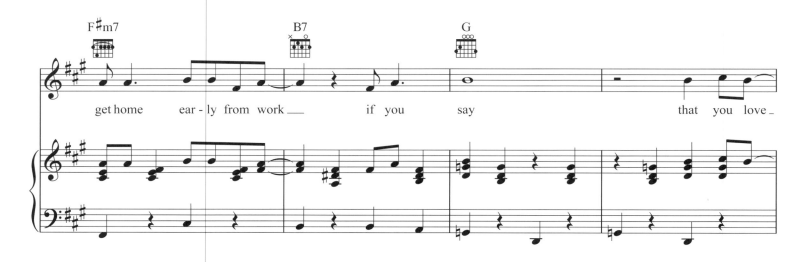

get home ear-ly from work ___ if you say that you love ___

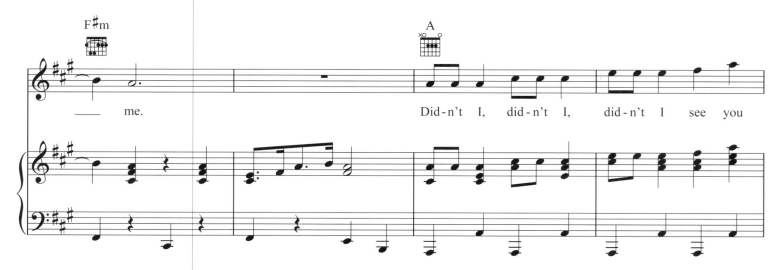

___ me. Did-n't I, did-n't I, did-n't I see you

cry - in' (cry - in', cry - in')? Oh, did - n't I, did - n't I, did - n't I see you

cry - in' (cry - in', cry - in')? Feel - in' all a - lone with - out a

friend, you know you feel like dy - in'. _____ Oh,

D.S. al Coda

did - n't I, did - n't I, did - n't I see you cry - in' (cry - in', cry - in')? I

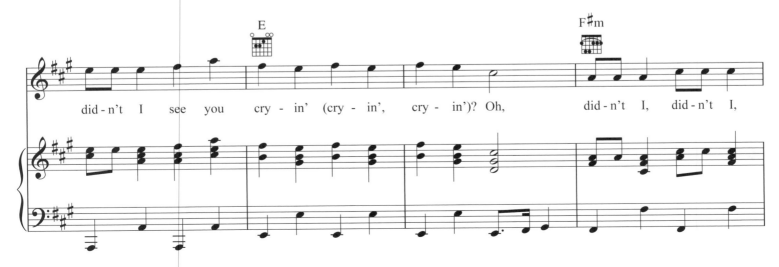

did-n't I see you cry-in' (cry-in', cry-in')? Feel-in' all a-lone with-out a

friend, you know you feel like dy - in' (dy - in', dy - in'). Oh,

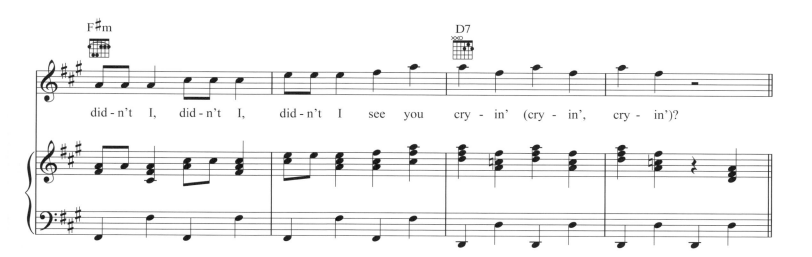

did-n't I, did-n't I, did-n't I see you cry-in' (cry-in', cry-in')?

Guitar solo

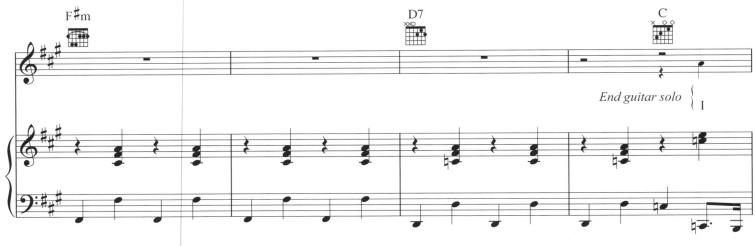

Feel-in' all a-lone with-out a friend, you know you feel like dy-in'. _____

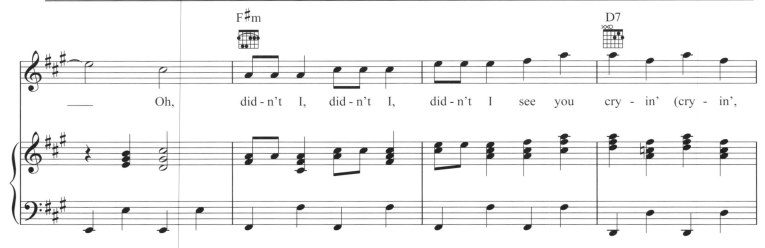

_____ Oh, did-n't I, did-n't I, did-n't I see you cry-in' (cry-in',

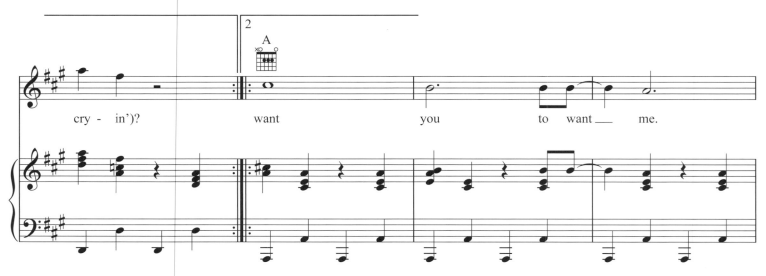

cry-in')? want you to want _____ me.

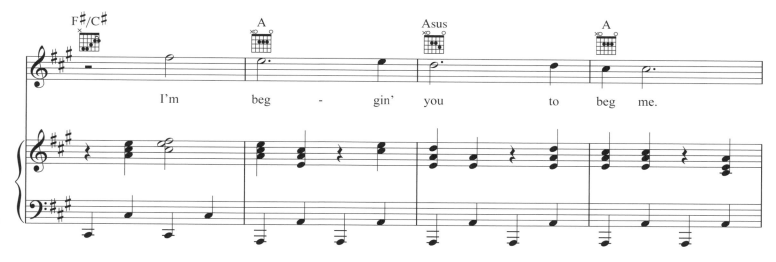

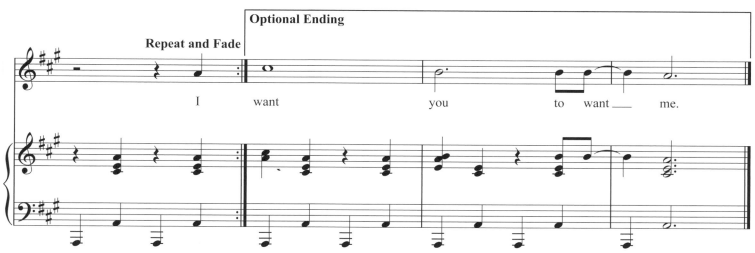

I'M A BELIEVER

Words and Music by
NEIL DIAMOND

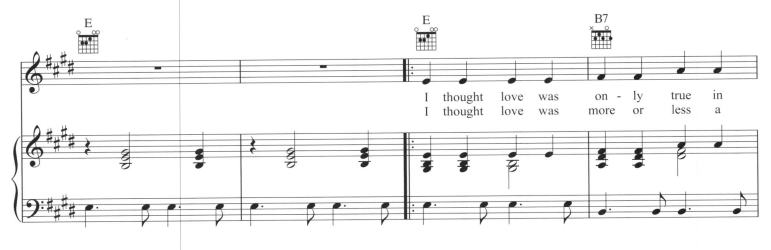

I thought love was on - ly true in
I thought love was more or less a

fair - y tales,   meant for some - one else but not for
giv - in' thing;   seems the more I gave the less I

me.   Love was out to get me.
got.   (2., D.S.) What's the use in try - in'?

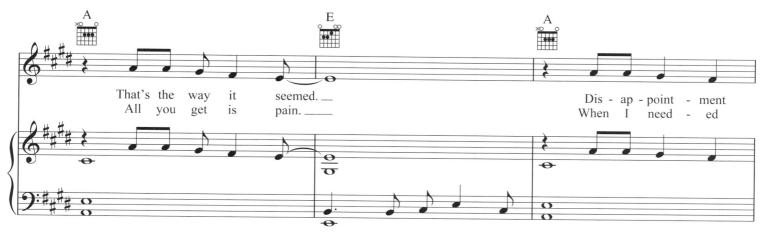

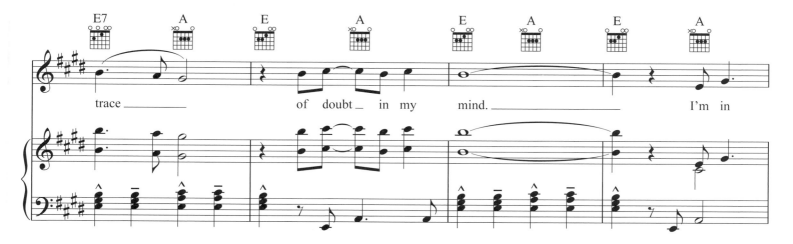

love,   and I'm a be - liev - er! I could - n't

leave her if I tried.

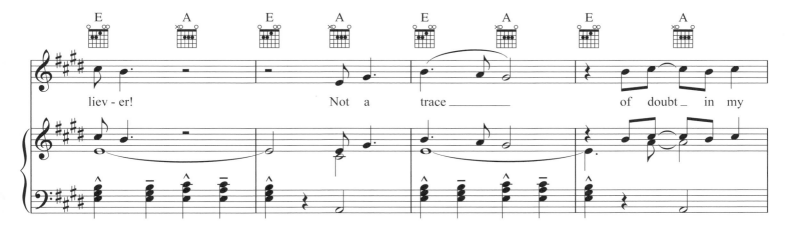

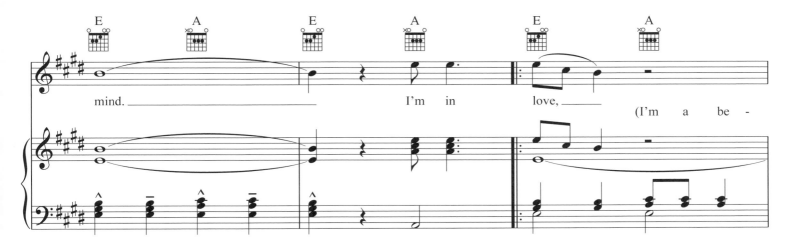

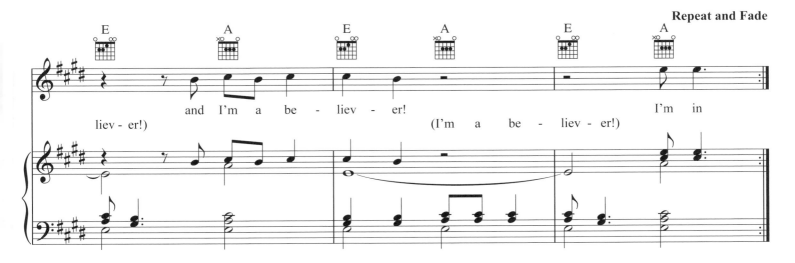

IN THE AIR TONIGHT

Words and Music by
PHIL COLLINS

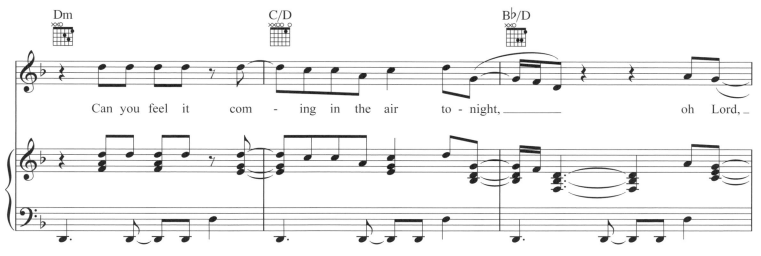

Can you feel it com - ing in the air to - night, _____ oh Lord, _

_____ oh Lord? _____

Well, if you told me _____ you were

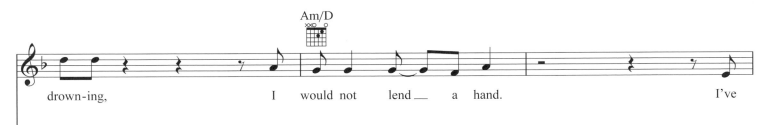

drown-ing, I would not lend _____ a hand. I've

seen your face __ be - fore, __ my friend, but I don't know if you know __ who I am. __

__ Well, I was there __ and I saw __ what you did. I

saw it with my own two eyes. __ So you can wipe off that grin. I

know where you've been. _____ It's all been a pack __ of lies.

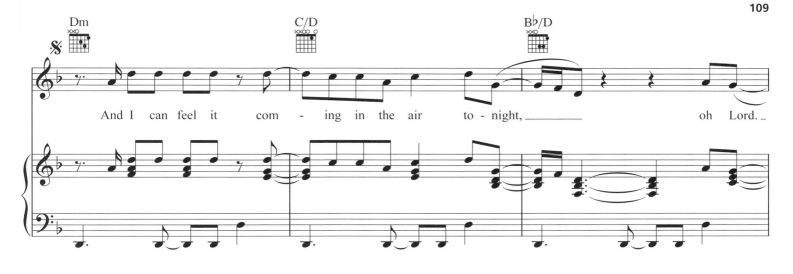

And I can feel it com - ing in the air to - night, _____ oh Lord. _

Well, I've been wait-ing for this mo-ment for all my life, _

_____ oh Lord. _____ I can feel it com -

- ing in the air to - night, _____ oh Lord. _____

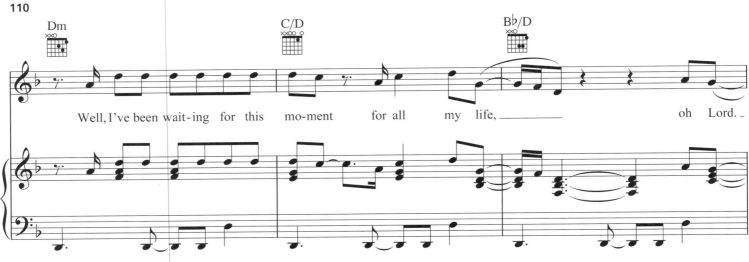

Well, I've been wait-ing for this mo-ment for all my life, _____ oh Lord. _

_____ oh Lord. _____

Well, I re - mem - ber, I re -

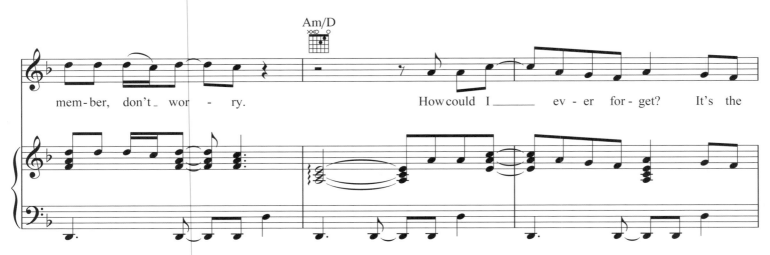

mem - ber, don't _ wor - ry. How could I _____ ev - er for - get? It's the

first time, __ the last time __ we ev - er met.

But I _____ know the rea - son __ why __ you keep the si - lence up.

No, you don't fool me. The hurt does - n't show, but the

D.S. and Fade

pain __ still grows. __ It's no stran - ger to you __ or me.

IRONIC

Lyrics by ALANIS MORISSETTE
Music by ALANIS MORISSETTE
and GLEN BALLARD

death row ___ par-don ___ two min-utes too ___ late.
plane crashed ___ down, he thought, "Well, is-n't this ___ nice..."
meet-ing the man of my dreams, and then

Is-n't it i-

- ron-ic... ___ don't you think? It's like rain ___

on your wed-ding ___ day. It's a free ___ ride ___

when you've al-read-y paid. It's the good ad-vice ___

And life has a fun - ny way ___ of help-ing you out ___

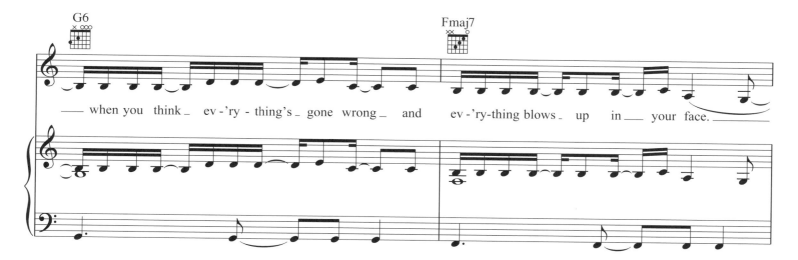

___ when you think ___ ev-'ry-thing's ___ gone wrong ___ and ev-'ry-thing blows ___ up in ___ your face. ___

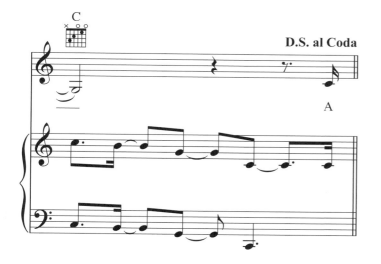

D.S. al Coda

A

CODA

meet-ing his beau - ti - ful wife.

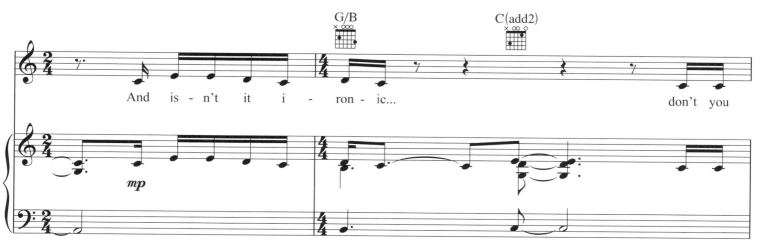

And is - n't it i - ron - ic... don't you

mp

think?   A lit - tle too i - ron - ic...   and yeah, I

real - ly do think...   it's like rain _____   on your

wed - ding _____ day.   It's a free ____ ride _____   when you've

al - read - y paid.   It's the good ad - vice _____   that you

just did-n't take. _ And who would have thought, _ it fig-ures. _

And _ you know life has a fun-ny way of sneak-ing up on

you. _ Life has a fun-ny, fun-ny way _ of _ help-ing _ you out, _

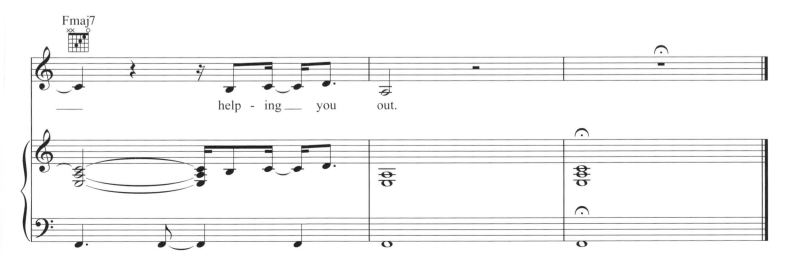

_ help - ing _ you out.

JACK AND DIANE

Words and Music by
JOHN MELLENCAMP

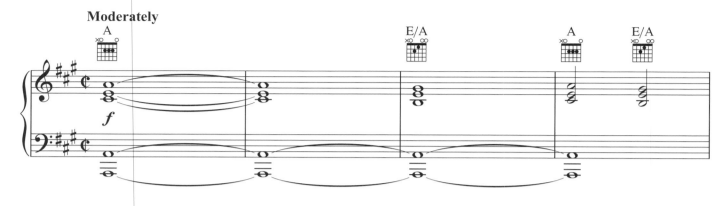

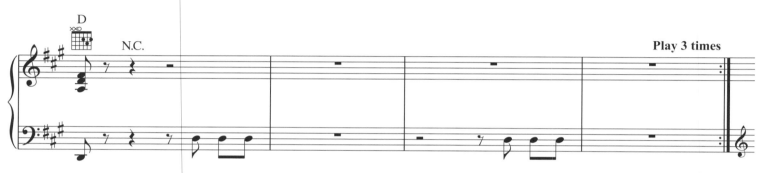

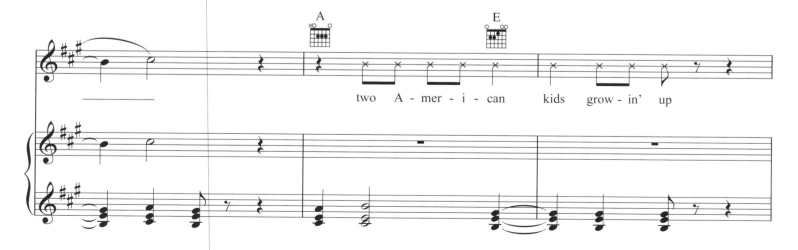

in the heart - land.   Jack, he's gon - na be ____

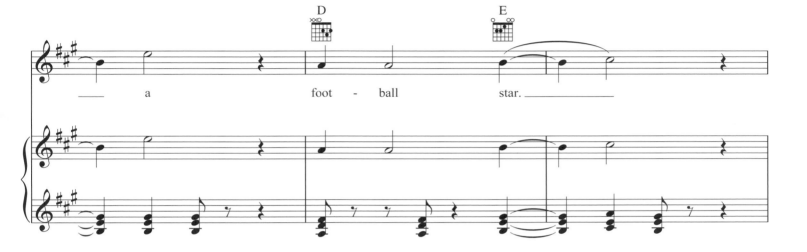

____ a   foot - ball   star. _____

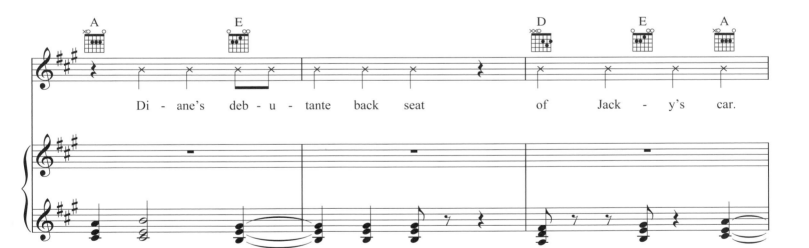

Di - ane's deb - u - tante back seat   of Jack - y's car.

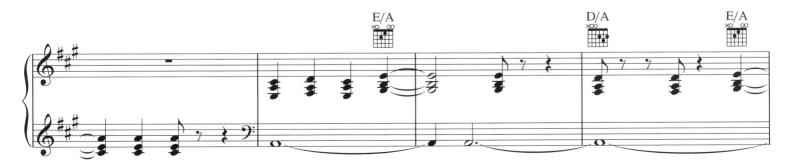

Jack, he says, "Hey, Di - ane, let's run off be - hind a shad - y tree; __
"Well, then, there, Di - ane, we got - ta run off to __ the cit -

_____ y."
Di - ane says, "Ba - by,

drib - ble off those Bob - bie Brooks. Let me
Let you ain't

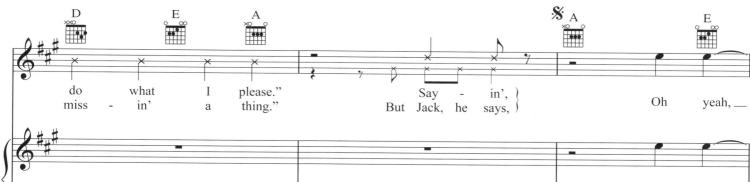

do what I please."
miss - in' a thing." But Jack, he says,
Say - in', }
Oh yeah, __

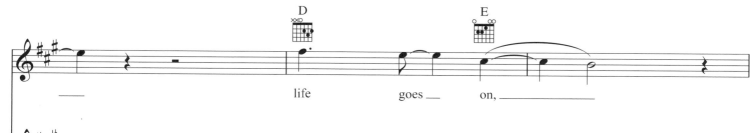

life goes __ on, _____

long af - ter the thrill of liv - ing is _____ gone. _____

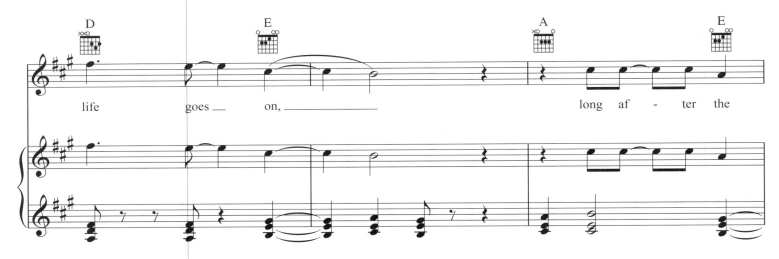

_____ Say - in', oh yeah, _____

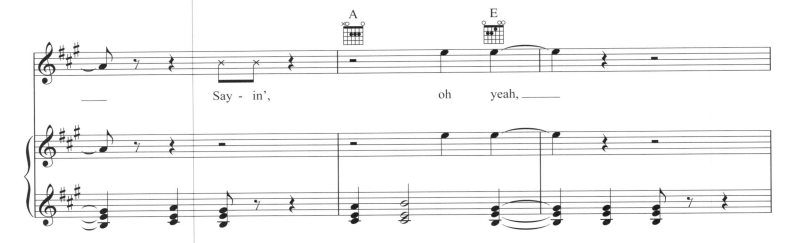

life goes _____ on, _____ long af - ter the

To Coda ⊕

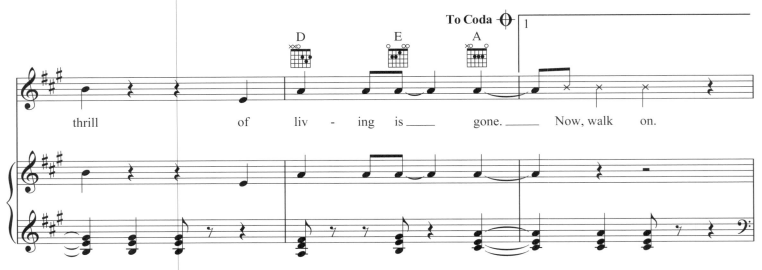

thrill of liv - ing is _____ gone. _____ Now, walk on.

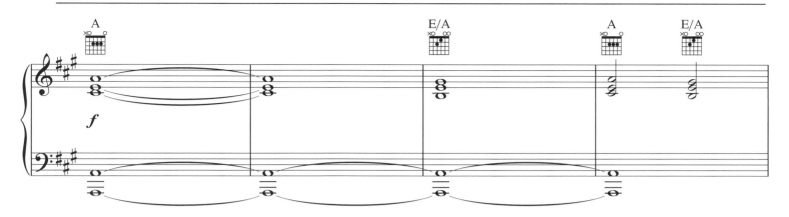

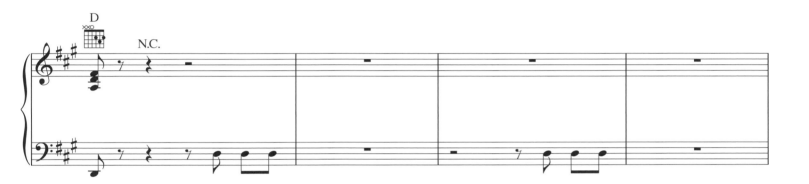

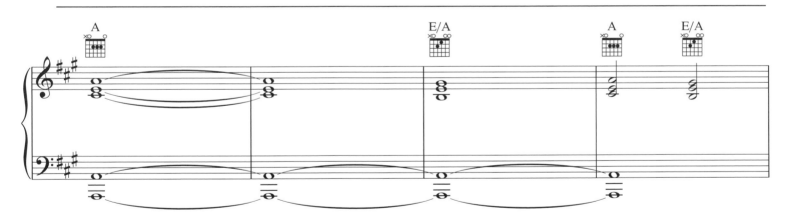

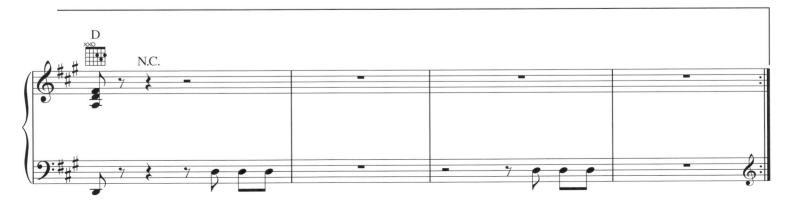

Oh, let it rock, let it roll, let the Bi - ble Belt come and save my soul. Hold - in' on to six - teen as long as you can;

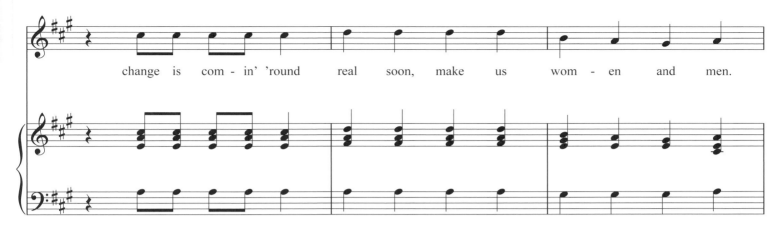

change is com- in' 'round real soon, make us wom- en and men.

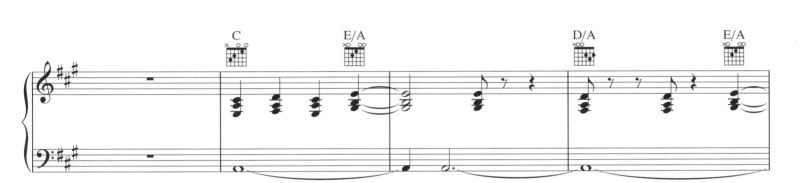

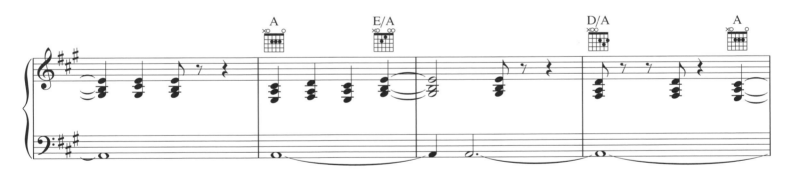

D.S. al Coda

CODA

A lit- tle

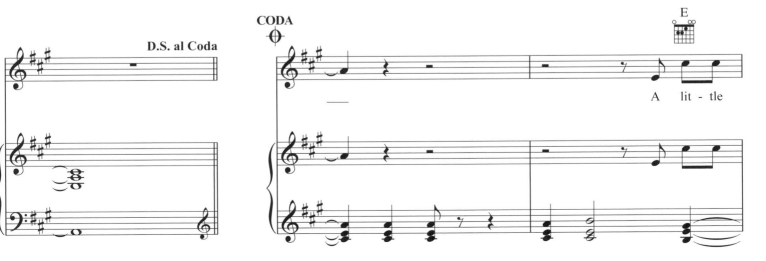

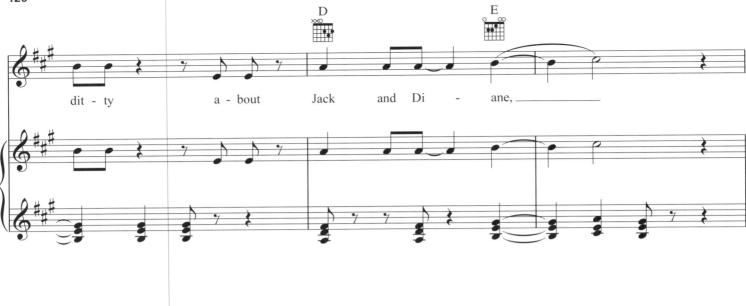

dit - ty   a - bout   Jack   and   Di - ane, _____

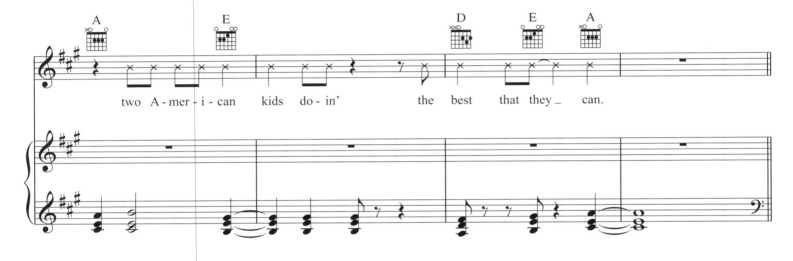

two A - mer - i - can   kids   do - in'   the   best   that they _ can.

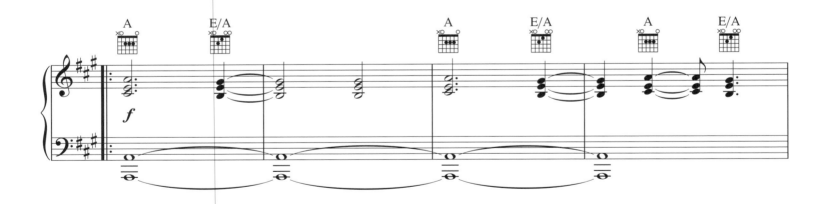

Repeat and Fade

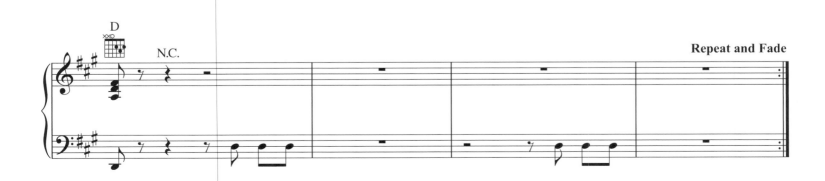

MY SHARONA

Words and Music by DOUG FIEGER
and BERTON AVERRE

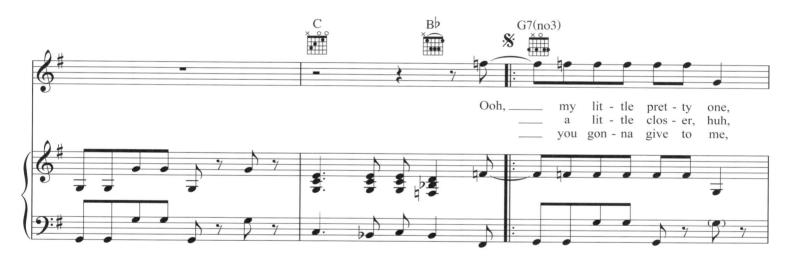

Ooh, _____ my lit - tle pret - ty one,
_____ a lit - tle clos - er, huh,
_____ you gon - na give to me,

my pret - ty one. When _____ you gon - na give me some time, Sha - ro - na? Ooh, _
a - will ya, huh? Close _____ e - nough to look in my eyes, Sha - ro - na. Keep -
g - give to me? Is _____ it just a mat - ter of time, Sha - ro - na? Is _____

End solo

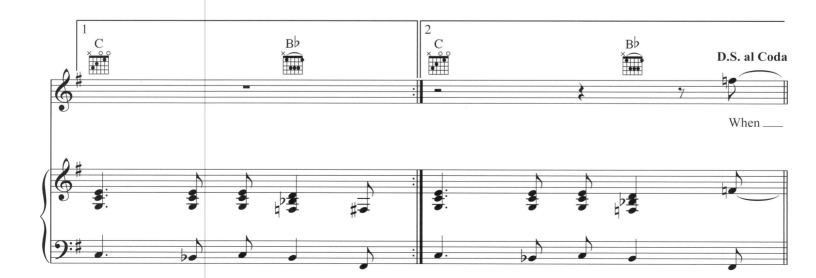

D.S. al Coda

When ___

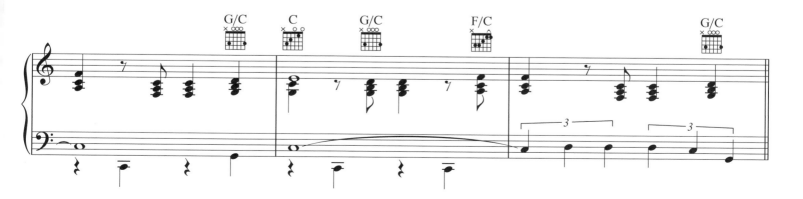

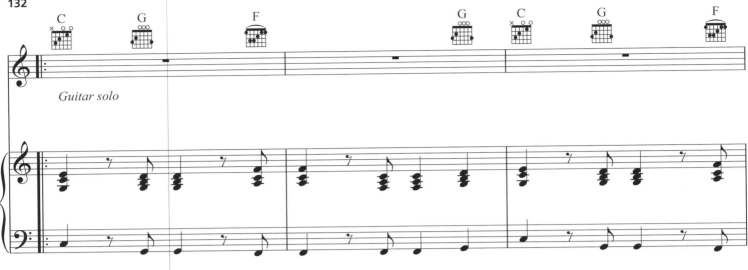

Guitar solo

Repeat ad lib.

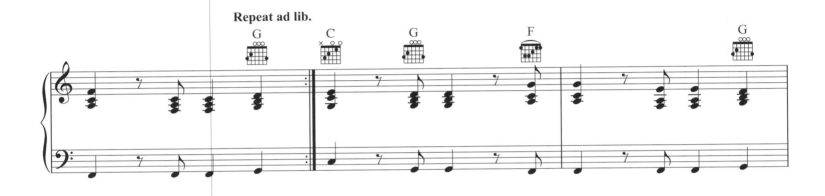

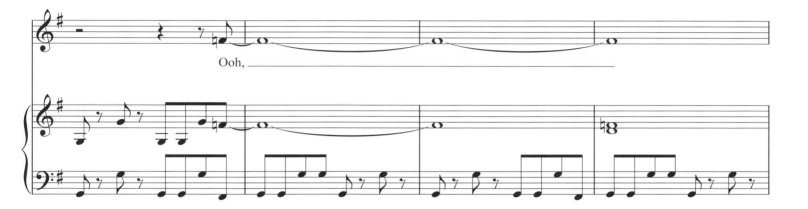

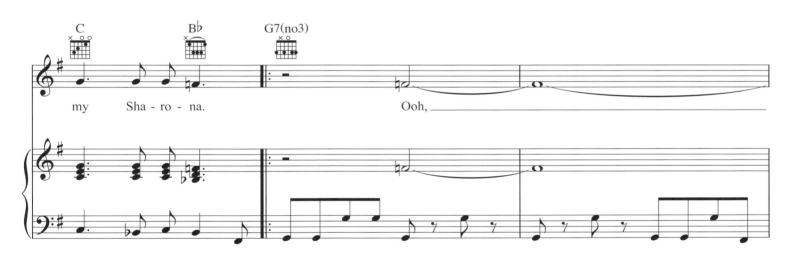

JESSIE'S GIRL

Words and Music by
RICK SPRINGFIELD

JUMP

Words and Music by EDWARD VAN HALEN,
ALEX VAN HALEN and DAVID LEE ROTH

Bright Rock

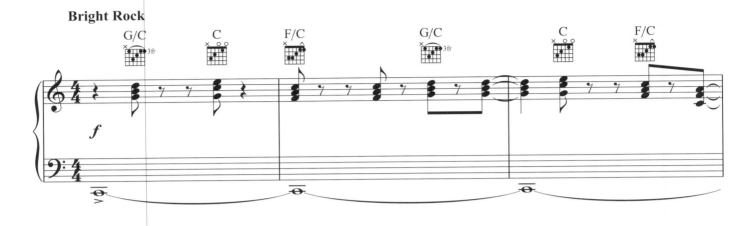

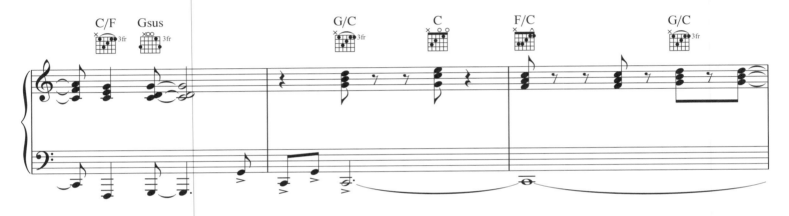

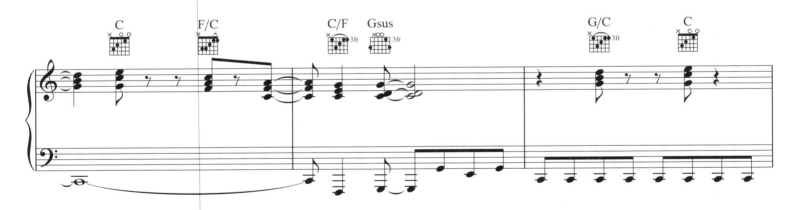

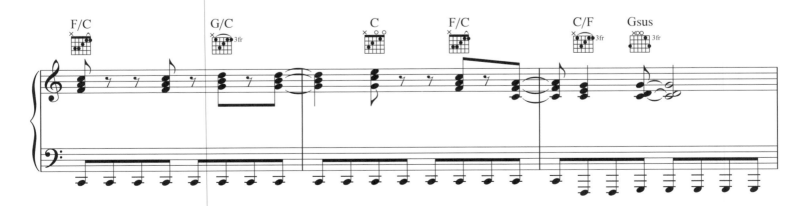

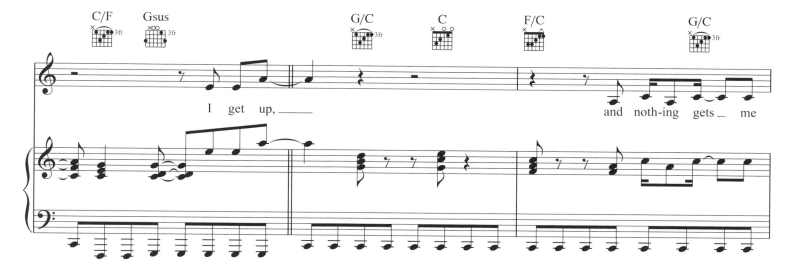

I get up, _____ and noth-ing gets _ me

down. You got it tough.

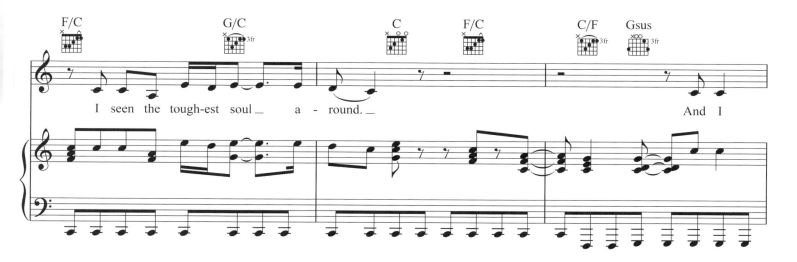

I seen the tough-est soul _ a - round. _ And I

know,　　　　　　　　　　ba-by, just___ how you　feel. __

You got to roll _____ with the punch-es　to get to what's

real. __　　　　　　　　　　　　　　Ah, can't you　see　me stand-ing here? I　got my

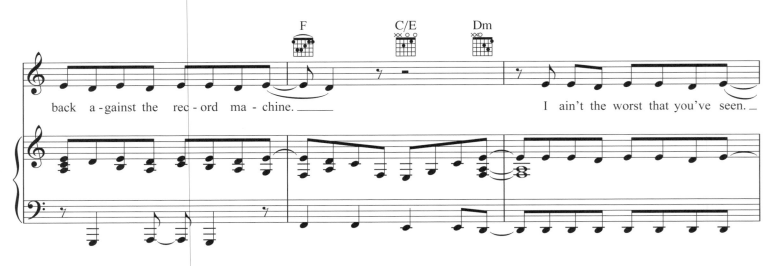

back a-gainst the rec-ord ma-chine. ____　　　　I ain't the worst that you've seen. __

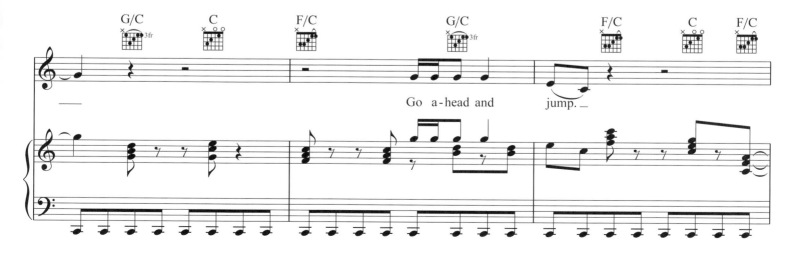

How old ____ are you? _ Who said that? ____ Ba-by, how _ you been? _

You say you don't know. _____ You won't

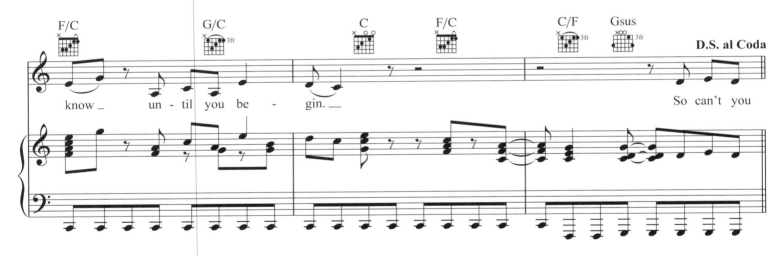

D.S. al Coda

know _ un-til you be - gin. _ So can't you

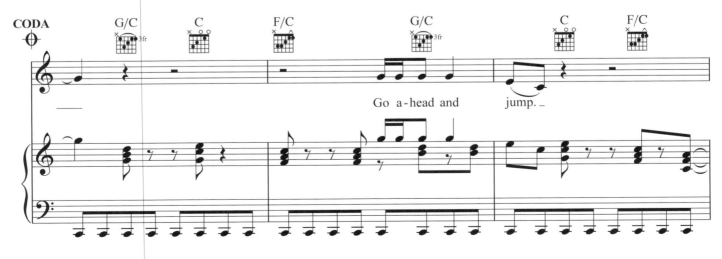

CODA

Go a-head and jump. _

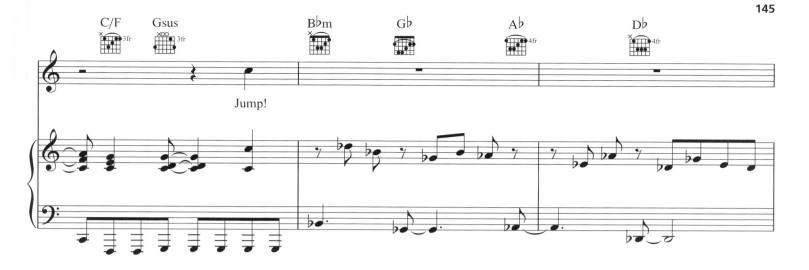

Jump!

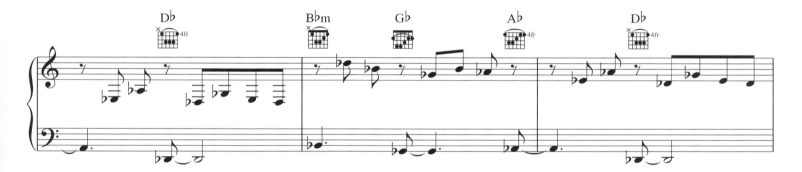

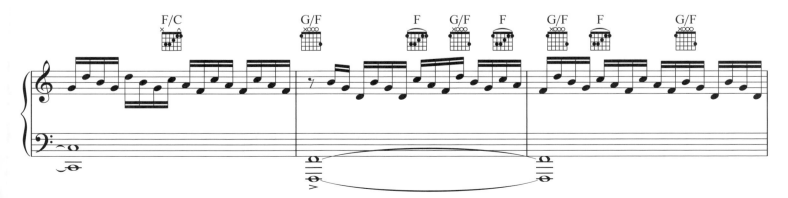

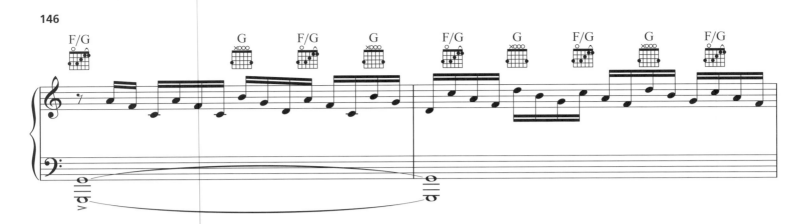

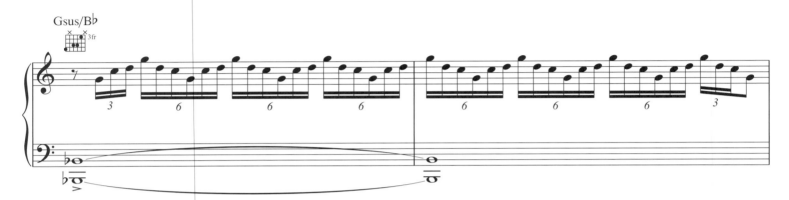

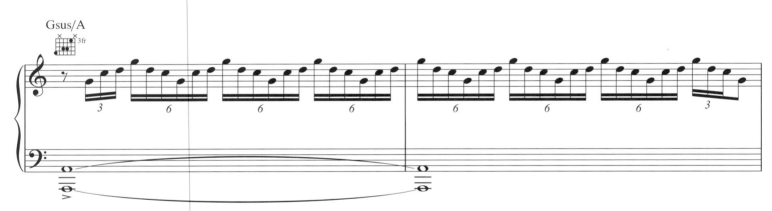

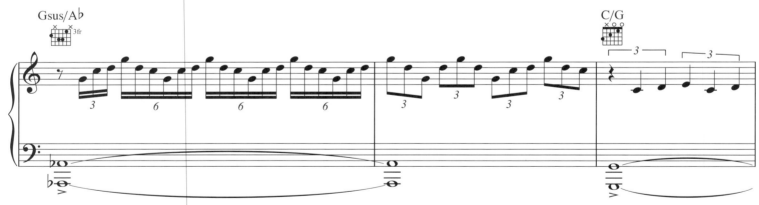

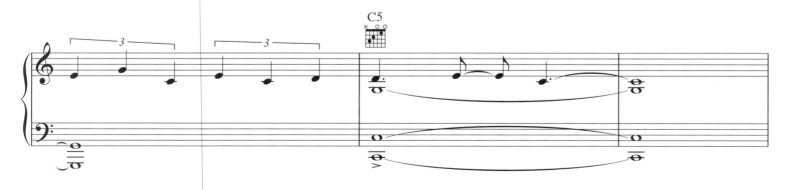

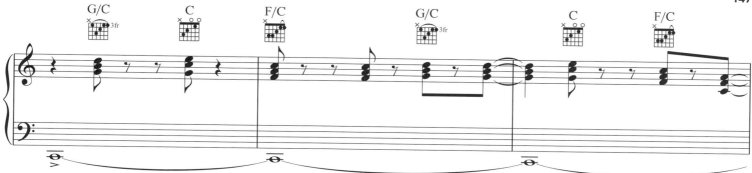

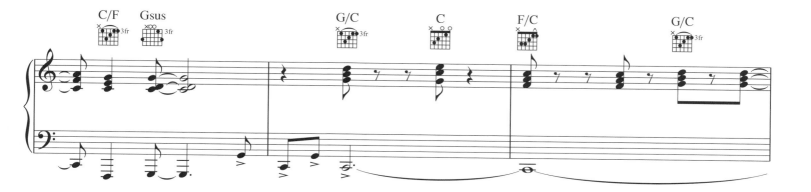

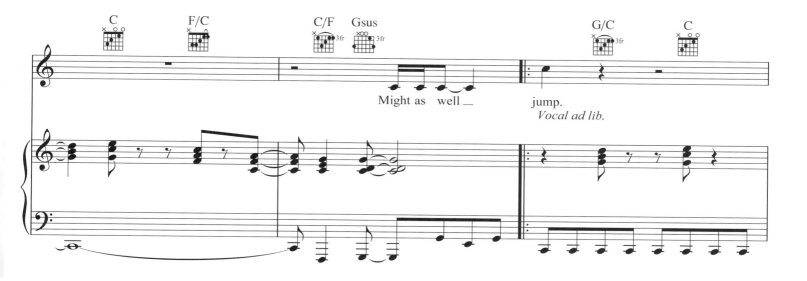

Might as well __ jump.
Vocal ad lib.

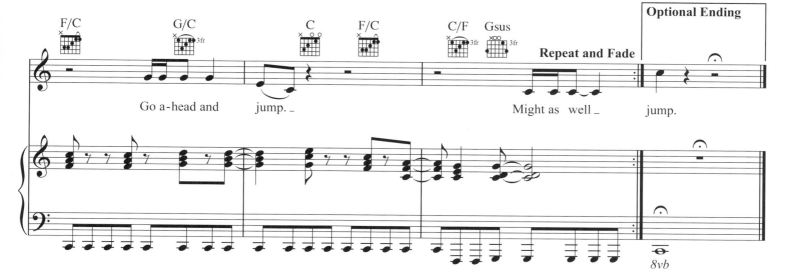

Repeat and Fade

Optional Ending

Go a-head and jump. __

Might as well __ jump.

8vb

JUST WHAT I NEEDED

Words and Music by
RIC OCASEK

Lyrics:

(1.,D.S.) I don't mind you com-ing here,
(2.) I don't mind you hang-ing out

wast-ing all my time.
and talk-ing in your sleep.

'Cause when you're stand-ing,
It does-n't mat-ter

oh, so ___ near,
where you've ___ been,

I kind of lose my mind.
as long as it was deep.

It's not the per - fume that you wear;
You al - ways knew to wear it well, and
it's not the rib - bons
you look so fan - cy.

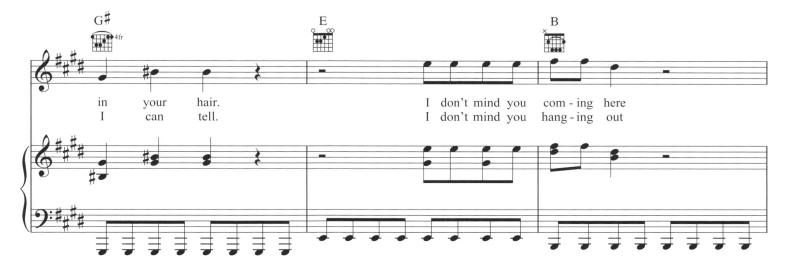

in your hair.
I can tell.
I don't mind you com - ing here
I don't mind you hang - ing out

and wast - ing all my time.
and talk - ing in your sleep.

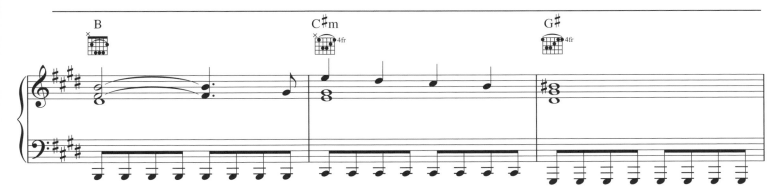

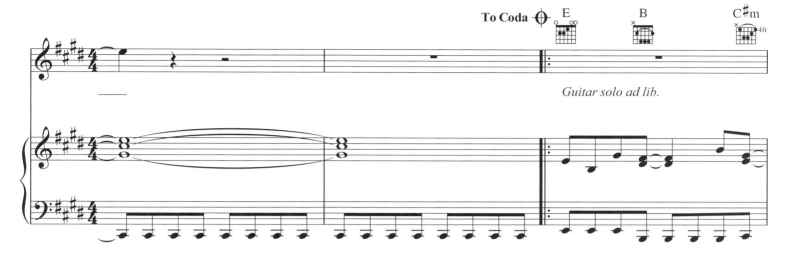

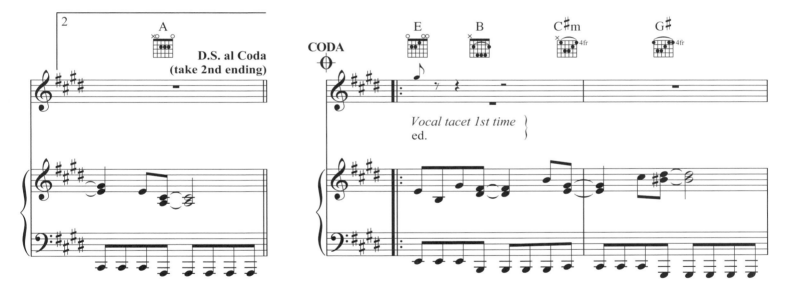

LIVIN' ON A PRAYER

Words and Music by JON BON JOVI,
DESMOND CHILD and RICHIE SAMBORA

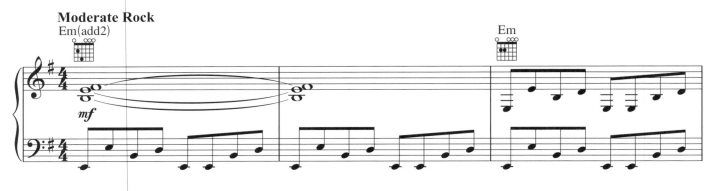

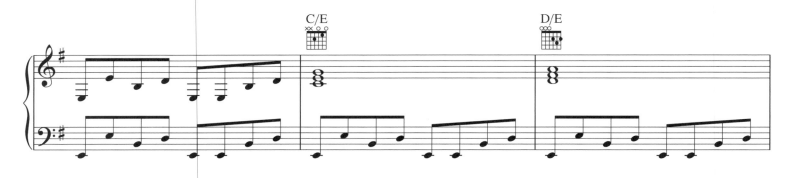

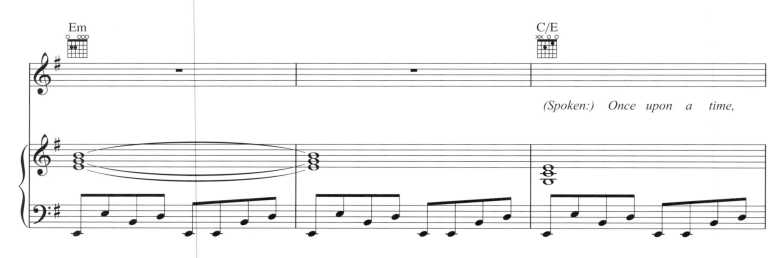

(Spoken:) Once upon a time,

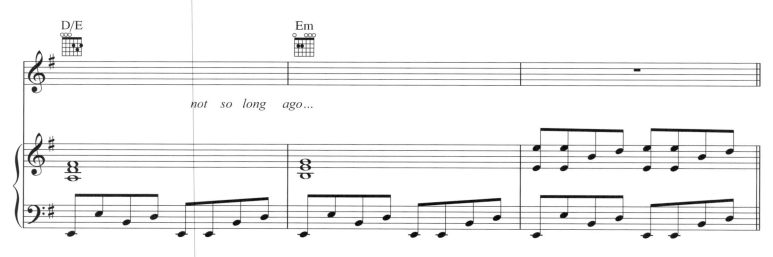

not so long ago...

Em

Tom - my used to work on the docks. _____ Un-ion's been on strike. He's
Tom-my's got his six-string in hock. _____ Now he's hold-ing in what he

Em(add2)   Em

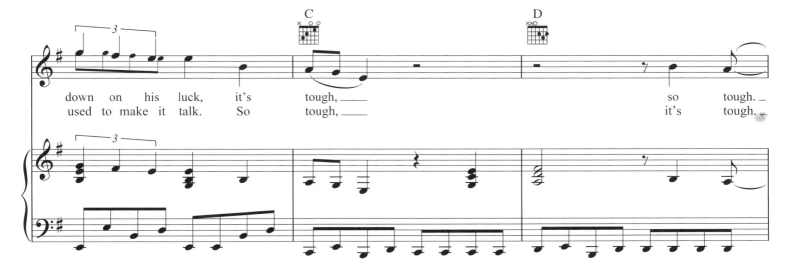

down on his luck, it's tough, _____ so tough. _
used to make it talk. So tough, _____ it's tough. _

C   D

Em

_____ Gi - na works the din - er all day. _
_____ Gi - na dreams of run - ning a - way. _

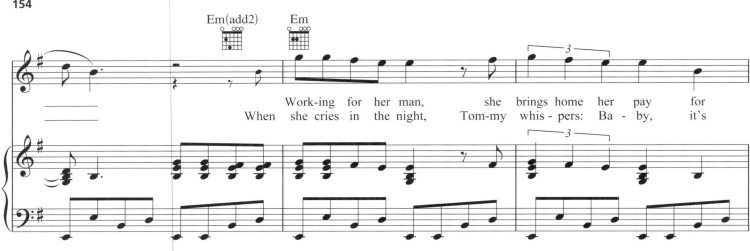

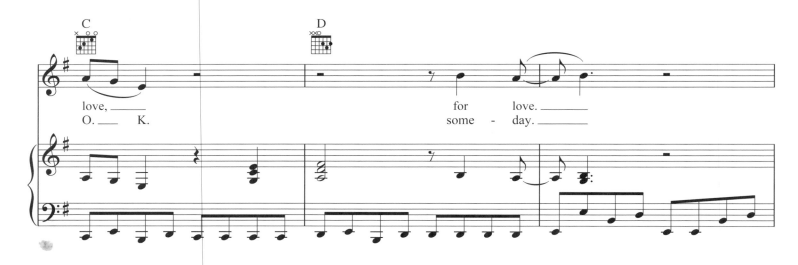

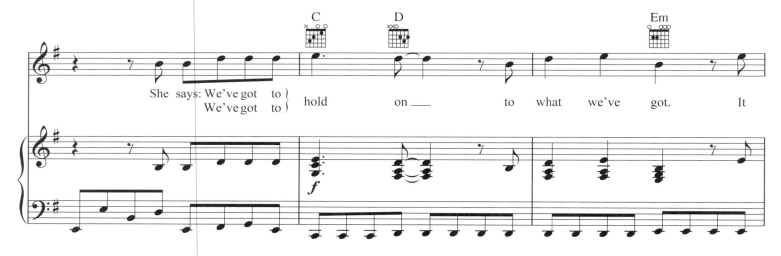

that's a lot for ___ love. ___ We'll give it a shot.

Whoa, ___ we're half - way there. ___ Whoa, ___ liv -

- in' on a prayer. ___ Take my ___ hand, ___ we'll make it, I ___ swear. ___

Whoa, ___ liv - in' on a prayer. ___

Liv - in' on ___ a prayer. ___

Instrumental

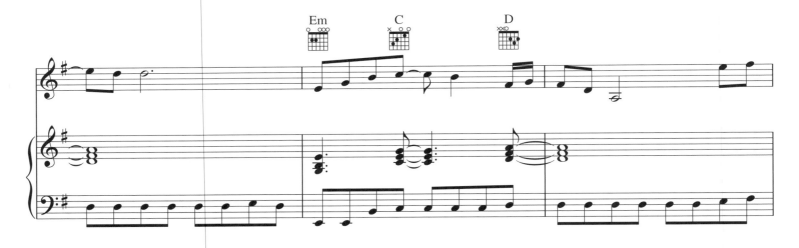

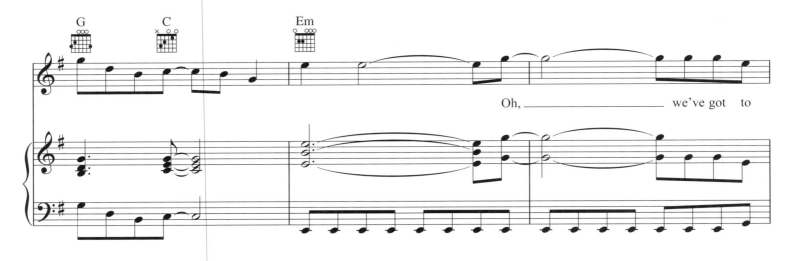

Oh, _____ we've got to

LOVE SHACK

Words and Music by CATHERINE E. PIERSON,
FREDERICK W. SCHNEIDER, KEITH J. STRICKLAND
and CYNTHIA L. WILSON

Moderate Rock

head - ed down   the At - lan - ta _____ high - way,

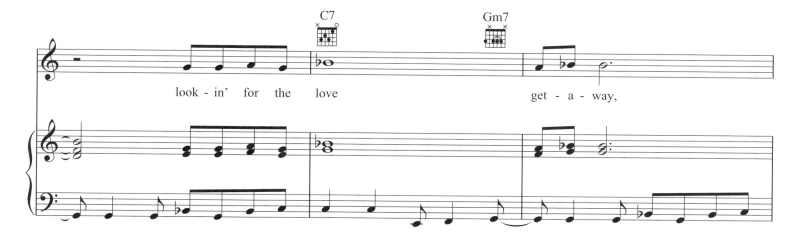

look - in' for the love   get - a - way,

head - in' ___ for the love _____ get - a - way. I   got me a car. ___ It's as
Hop in my Chry - sler,   it's as

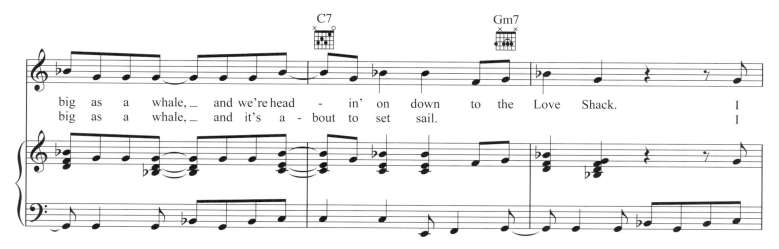

big as a whale, __ and we're head - in' on   down   to the Love Shack.   I
big as a whale, __ and it's a - bout to   set   sail.   I

got me a Chry - sler, it seats a - bout twen - ty. So, hur - ry up and bring your
got me a car, ____ it seats a - bout twen - ty. So, come on and bring your

juke - box mon - ey. } The Love Shack _ is a lit - tle old place where
juke - box mon - ey.

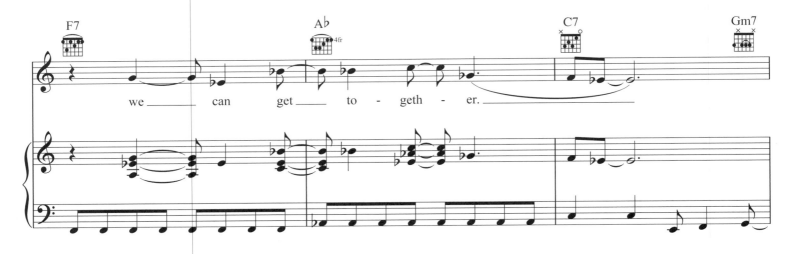

we ____ can get ___ to - geth - er. ____

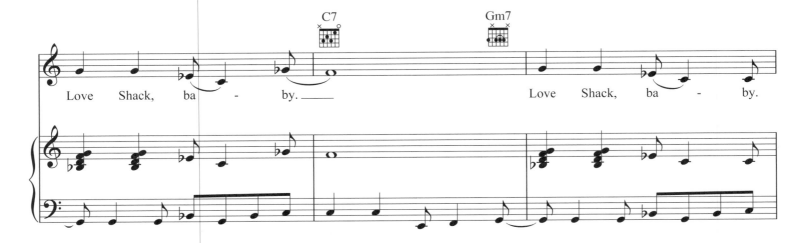

Love Shack, ba - by. ___ Love Shack, ba - by.

Love Shack, ba - by, Love ___ Shack, Love Shack, ba - by, Love __

To Coda ⊕

__ Shack, Love Shack, ba - by, Love __ Shack,

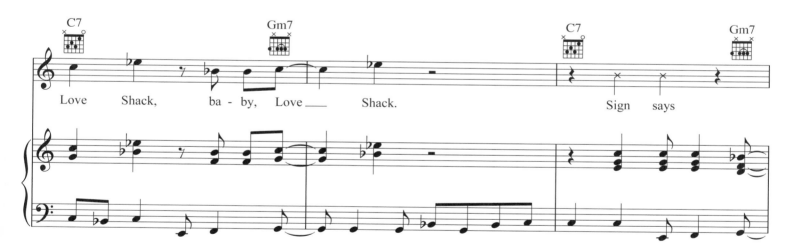

Love Shack, ba - by, Love __ Shack. Sign says

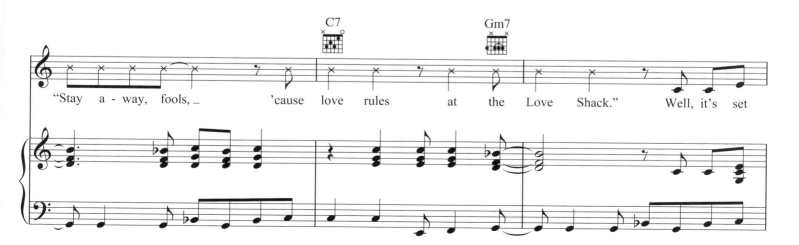

"Stay a - way, fools, __ 'cause love rules at the Love Shack." Well, it's set

way back in the mid-dle of a field. __ Just a funk-y old shack and I

got-ta get back. _____ Glit-ter on the mat-tress, _____

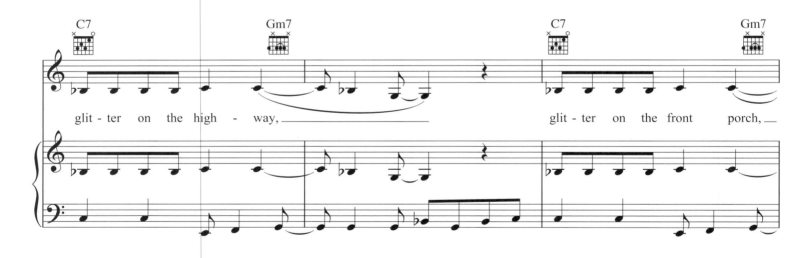

glit-ter on the high-way, _____ glit-ter on the front porch, __

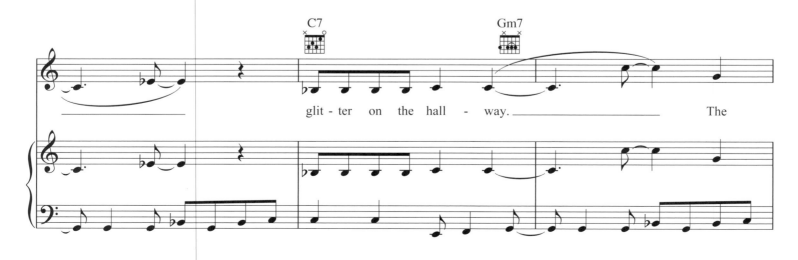

_____ glit-ter on the hall-way. _____ The

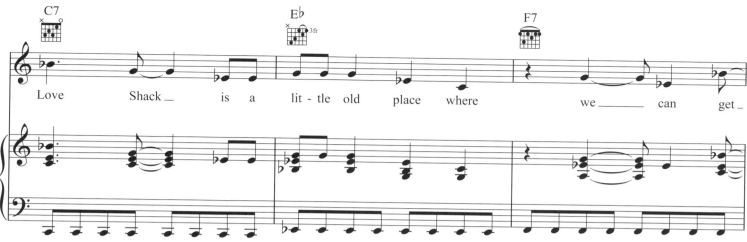

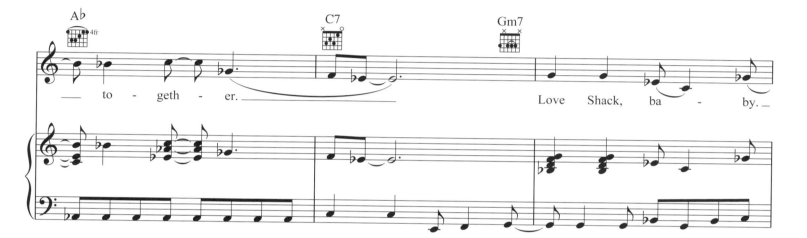

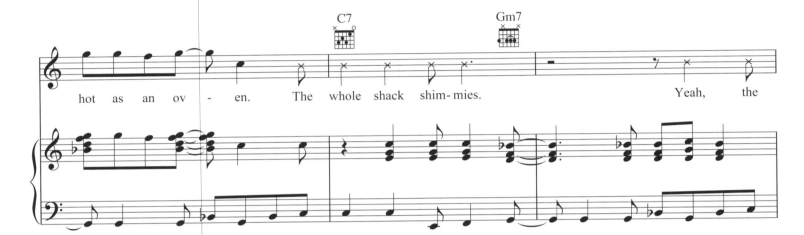

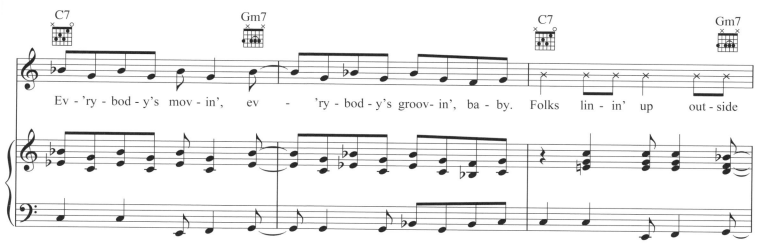

Ev -'ry - bod - y's mov - in', ev - 'ry - bod - y's groov - in', ba - by. Folks lin - in' up out - side

just to get down. Ev -'ry - bod - y's mov - in', ev - 'ry - bod - y's groov - in', ba - by.

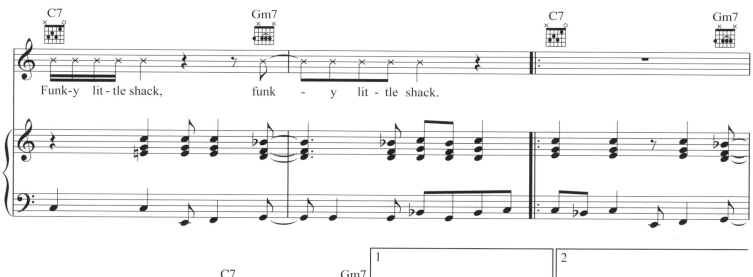

Funk-y lit - tle shack, funk - y lit - tle shack.

D.S. al Coda

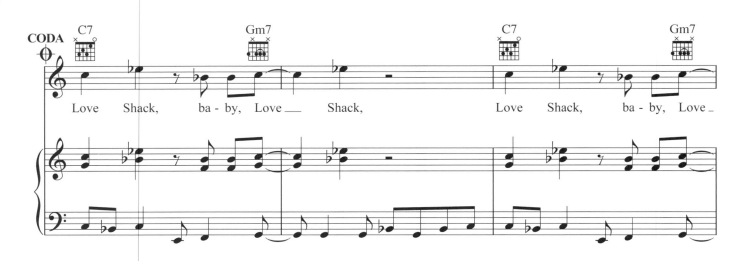

CODA

C7   Gm7   C7   Gm7

Love Shack, ba - by, Love ___ Shack,   Love Shack, ba - by, Love _

N.C.

___ Shack.

C7   Gm7   C7   Gm7

1–3

Bang, bang, _ bang   on the door, ba - by.

Knock a lit - tle loud - er, ba - by.
I can't   hear   you.
Knock a lit - tle loud - er, sug - ar.

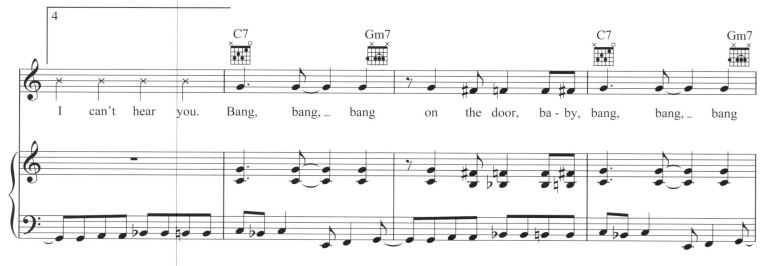

4

C7   Gm7   C7   Gm7

I can't hear you. Bang, bang, _ bang   on the door, ba - by, bang, bang, _ bang

on the door, ba-by. Bang, bang   on the door,_ ba-by, bang, bang

on the door._   Your what? Tin___ roof rust-ed.

Love Shack, ba-by, Love___ Shack,   Love Shack, ba-by, Love_

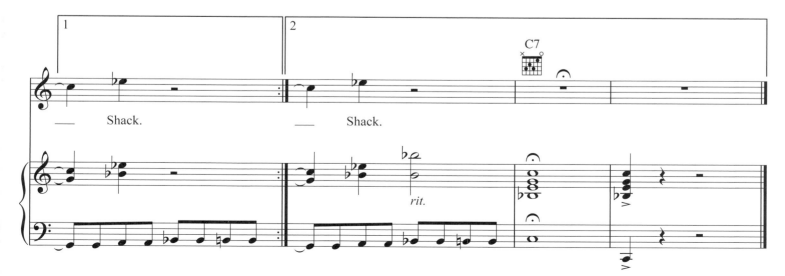

___ Shack.   ___ Shack.

rit.

MISS YOU

Words and Music by MICK JAGGER
and KEITH RICHARDS

Moderate Hard Rock beat

I been haul-in' ass __ so long. __ I been
howl-in' in __ my sleep. __ You been

Instrumental

sleep-in' all __ a - lone. __ Lord, I miss you!
star-in' in __ my dreams. __ Lord, I'll miss you to - night.

I been hang-in' on __ the phone. __ I been
I been wait-in' in __ the hall. __ I been

Instrumental ends (Spoken:) *I been walkin' Central Park,*

hoo hoo.
around, you know, like we used to!"
sometime I say...

Well, I been

Ooh, _____ ba - by, why you wait so long? _____

Ooh, _____ ba - by, why you wait so long? _

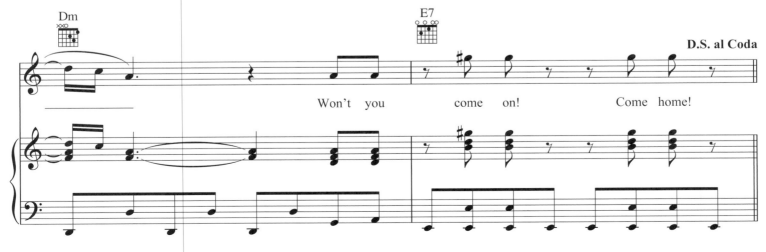

Won't you come on! Come home!

D.S. al Coda

CODA

Hoo hoo _ hoo _____ hoo _ hoo _ hoo. _____ I wan-na

kiss you, child. _ I guess I'm ly - in' to my - self. _ It's just

you, and no _ one else. _ Lord, _ I wan-na kiss you, child! _____ Hah _

Repeat and Fade

hah _ hah _____ hah _ hah _ hah _____ hah _____ hah. Hah _

MONY, MONY

Words and Music by BOBBY BLOOM,
TOMMY JAMES, RITCHIE CORDELL
and BO GENTRY

Hey, she give me lov - in', I feel _____ all right, _____ now. _____
Don't stop cook - in', it feels _____ so good, _ yeah. _____

(1.) You've got me

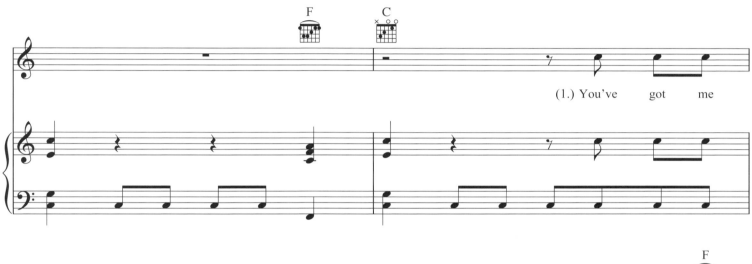

toss - in', turn - in' the mid - dle of the night, and I feel _____
Don't stop now. Come on, Mo - ny.

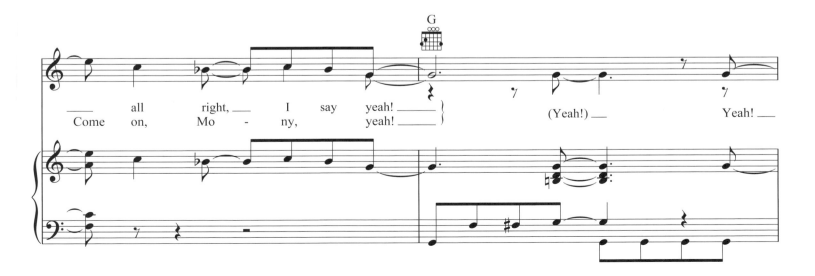

_____ all right, _____ I say yeah! _____
Come on, Mo - ny, yeah! _____
(Yeah!) _____
Yeah! _____

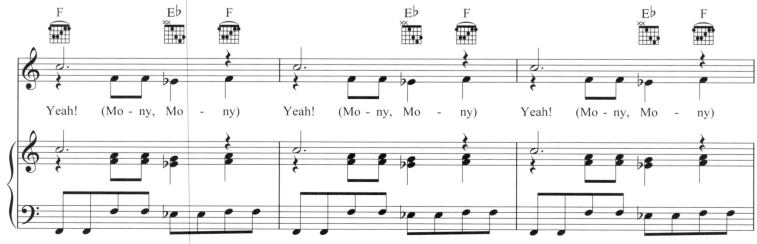

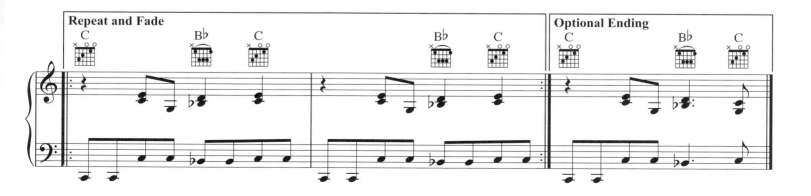

NO MATTER WHAT

Written by
PETER HAM

Medium Power Rock

Lyrics:

No mat-ter what you are, _____ I _____ will al-ways be with you.

Bm you.

Does-n't mat-ter what you do, _____ girl. _____

Ooh, _____ girl, _____ want you. _____

No mat-ter where you

go, ___ I ___ will al - ways be a - round. ___

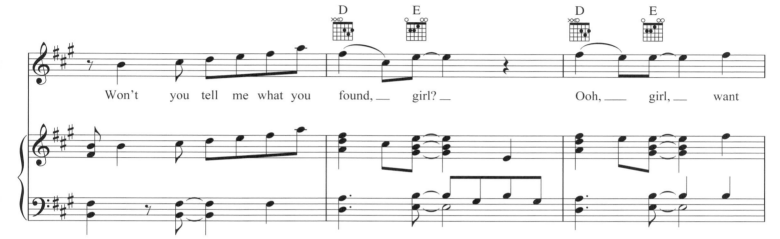

Won't you tell me what you found, ___ girl? ___ Ooh, ___ girl, ___ want

you. ___ Knock down the old gray

wall. Be a part ___ of it all. ___ Noth - ing to

say,   noth-ing to see, ___   noth-ing to do. ___

If you   would give   me all, ___   as

I   would give ___ it to ___ you,   noth-ing would be,   noth-ing would

be, ___   noth-ing would   be. ___   No mat-ter where   you
                                                                No mat-ter what   you

go, ___ there ___ will al - ways be a place. ___
are, ___ I ___ will al - ways be with you. ___

Can't you see it in my face, girl? ___ }
Does - n't mat - ter what you do, girl. ___ }

Ooh, ___ girl, ___ want

To Coda

you. ___

Guitar solo

OH, PRETTY WOMAN

Words and Music by ROY ORBISON
and BILL DEES

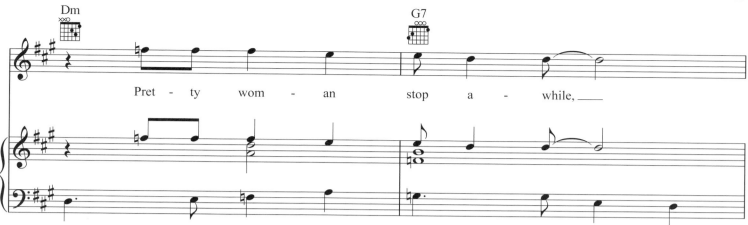

Pret - ty wom - an stop a - while, ___

Pret - ty wom - an talk a - while, _ Pret - ty wom - an

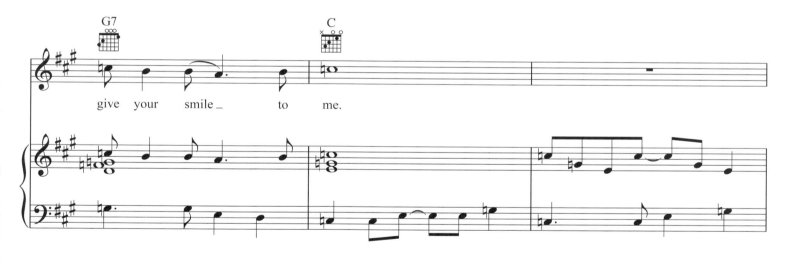

give your smile _ to me.

Pret - ty wom - an yeah, yeah, yeah, _____ Pret - ty wom - an

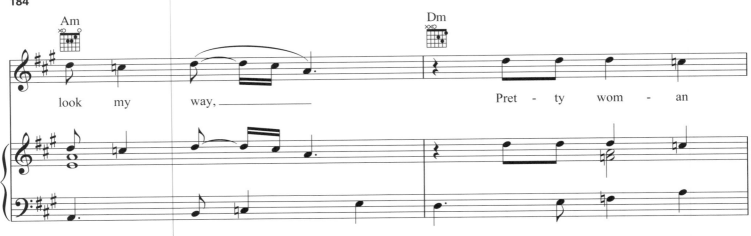

look my way, _____ Pret - ty wom - an

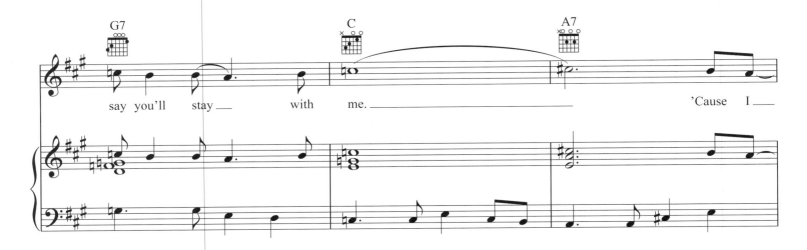

say you'll stay ___ with me. _____ 'Cause I ___

___ need you ___ I'll treat you right.

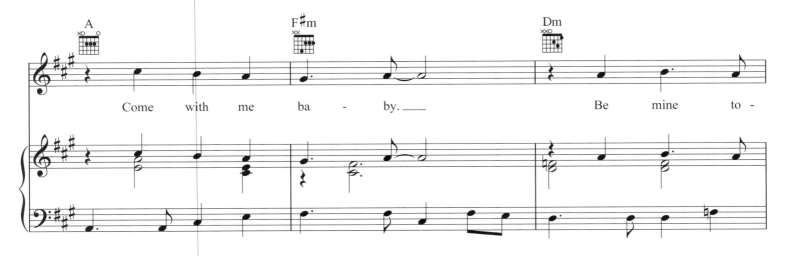

Come with me ba - by. ___ Be mine to -

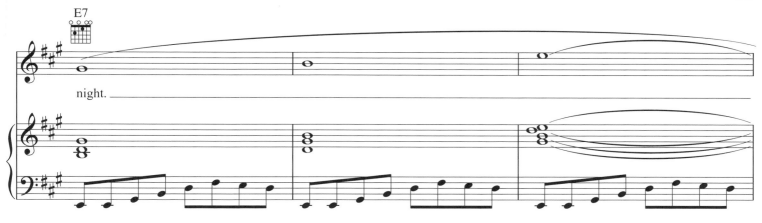

night.

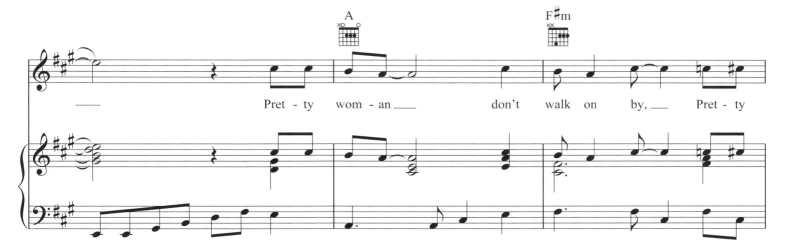

Pret - ty wom - an ____ don't walk on by, ___ Pret - ty

wom - an ____ don't make me cry, ____ Pret - ty

wom - an ____ don't walk a - way. ___

PARADISE BY THE
DASHBOARD LIGHT

Words and Music by
JIM STEINMAN

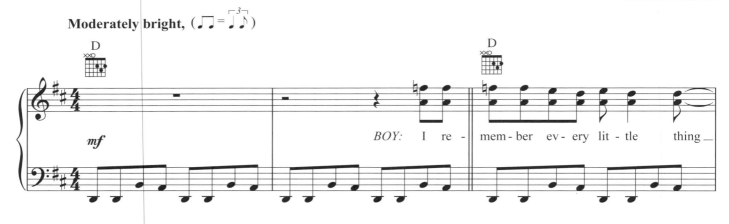

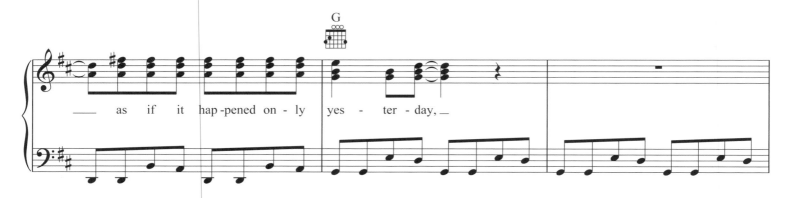

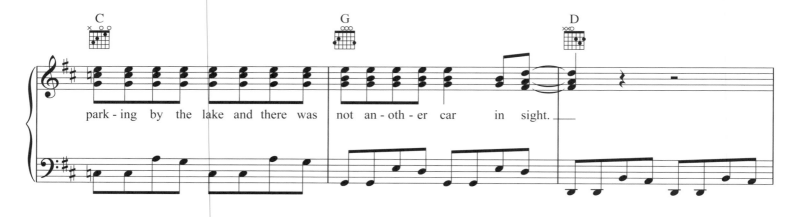

you did, and all the kids at school,_ they were

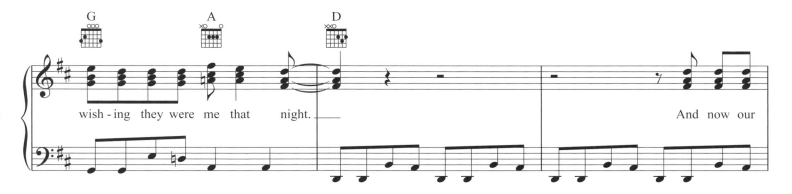

wish-ing they were me that night._ And now our

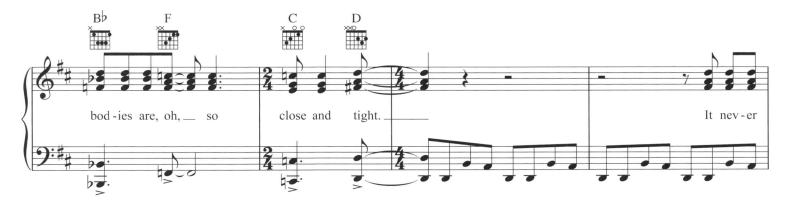

bod-ies are, oh,_ so close and tight._ It nev-er

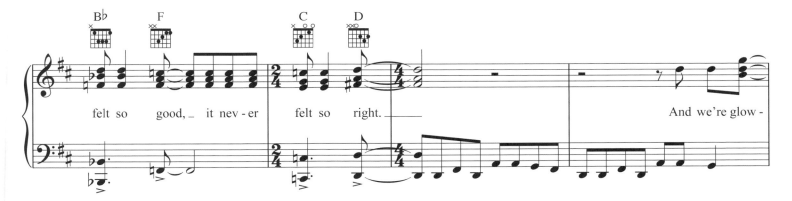

felt so good,_ it nev-er felt so right._ And we're glow -

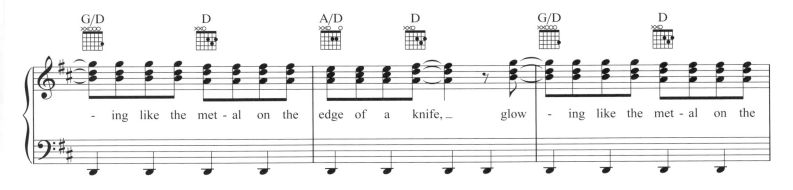

-ing like the met-al on the edge of a knife,_ glow -ing like the met-al on the

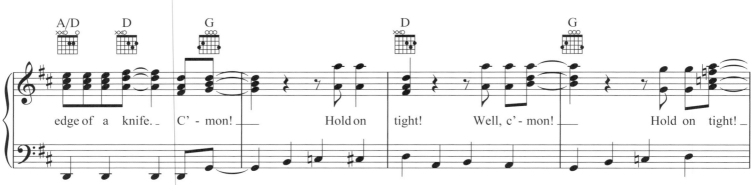

edge of a knife. ___ C'-mon! ___ Hold on tight! Well, c'-mon! ___ Hold on tight! ___

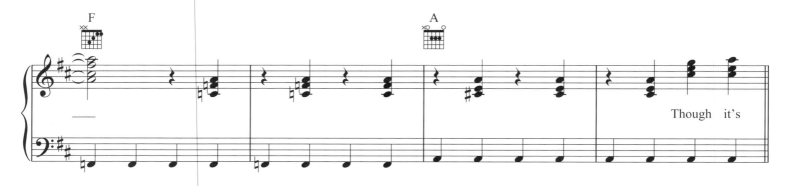

Though it's

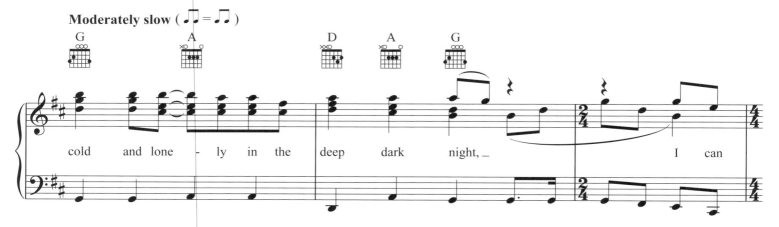

Moderately slow (♪♪ = ♪♪)

cold and lone - ly in the deep dark night, ___ I can

see par - a - dise ___ by the dash - board ___ light.

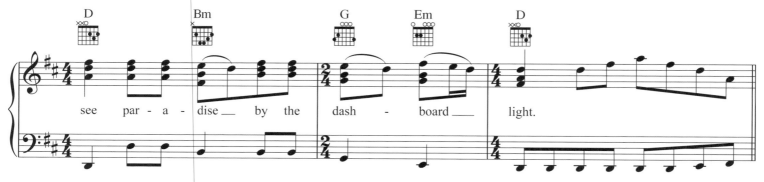

Tempo Primo (♪♪ = ♪♪)

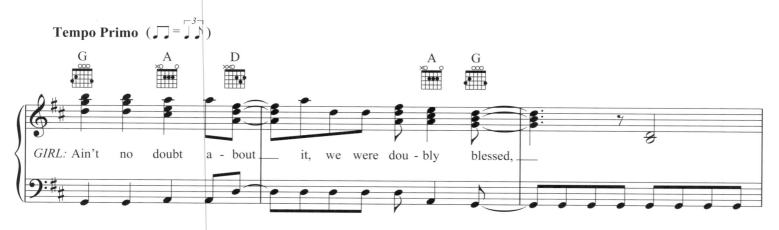

GIRL: Ain't no doubt a - bout ___ it, we were dou - bly blessed, ___

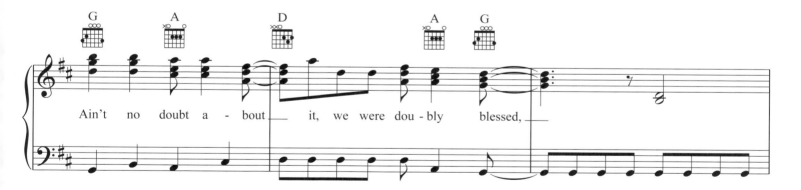

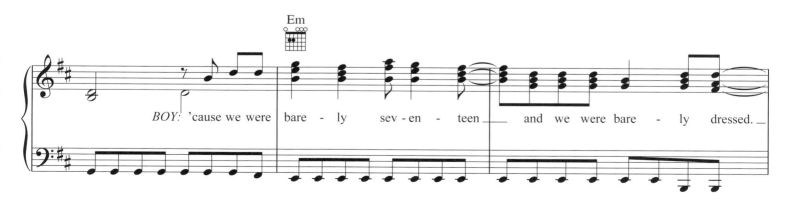

Ba - by, don't-cha hear my heart, you got it drown-ing out the ra - di - o.

I've been wait-ing so long for you to come a-long and have some fun.

And I got - ta let ya know, no,

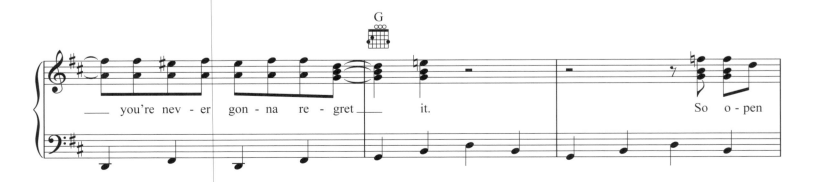

you're nev - er gon - na re - gret it. So o-pen

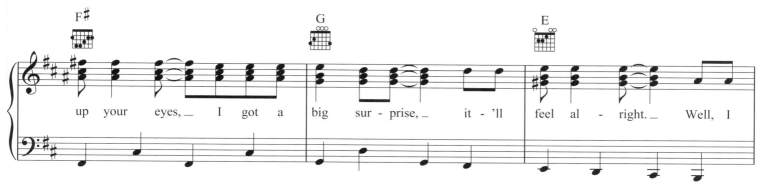

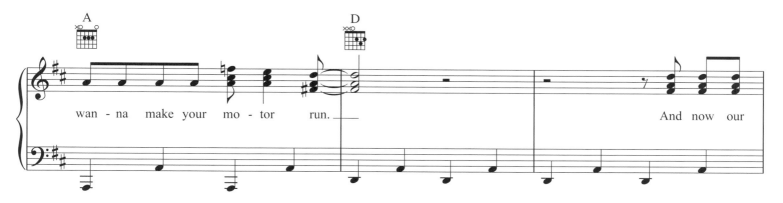

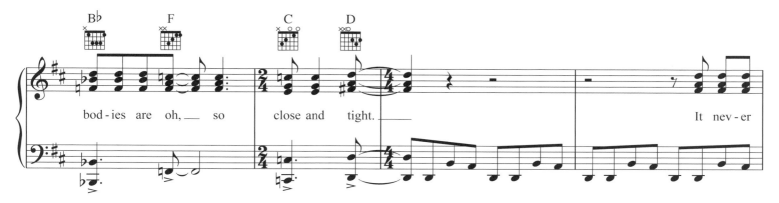

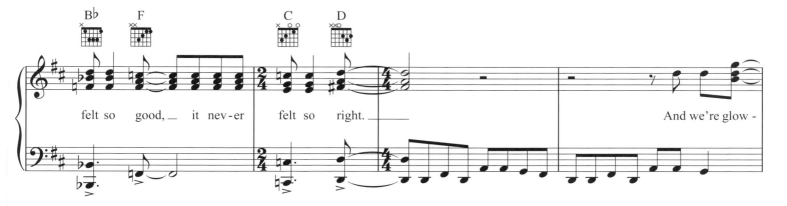

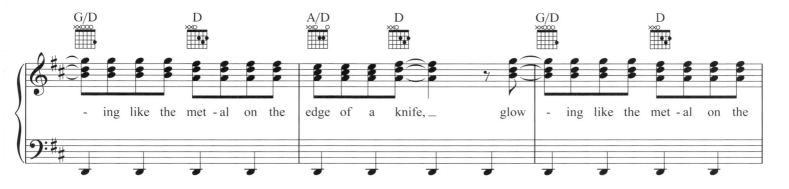

edge of a knife. ____ C'-mon! ____ Hold on tight! Well, c'-mon! ____

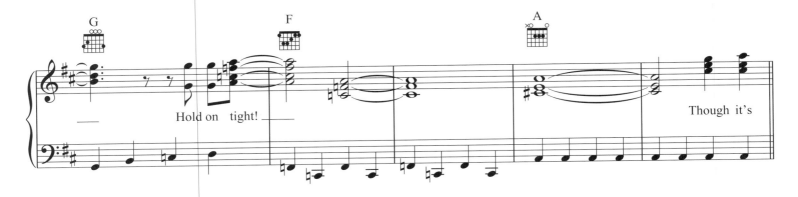

____ Hold on tight! Though it's

Moderately slow (♩♩ = ♩♩)

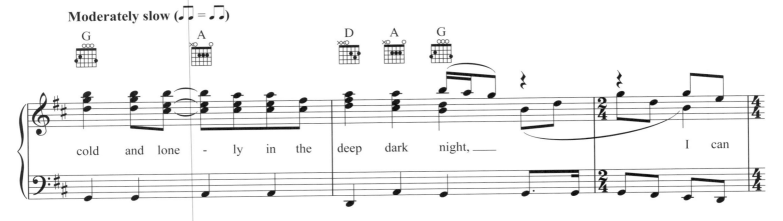

cold and lone-ly in the deep dark night, ____ I can

see par-a-dise by_ the dash-board light. ____ Though it's

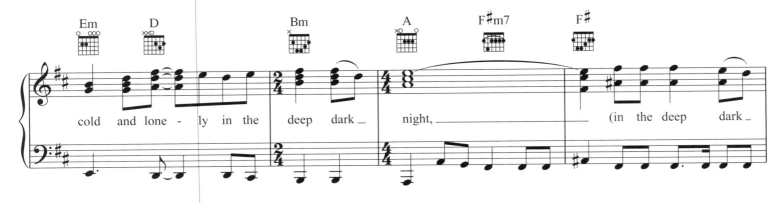

cold and lone-ly in the deep dark _ night, ____ (in the deep dark _

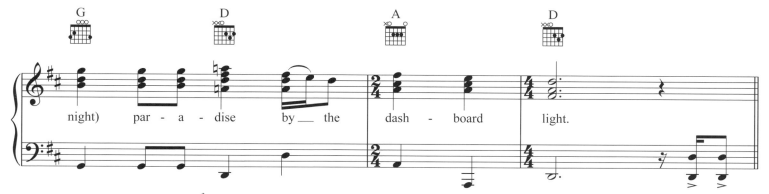

night) par - a - dise by — the dash - board light.

Tempo Primo

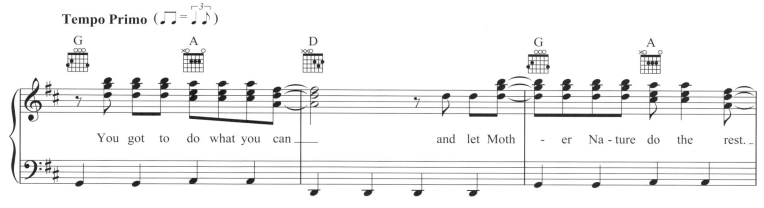

You got to do what you can — and let Moth - er Na - ture do the rest. —

— There ain't no doubt a - bout — it, we were dou - bly blessed, —

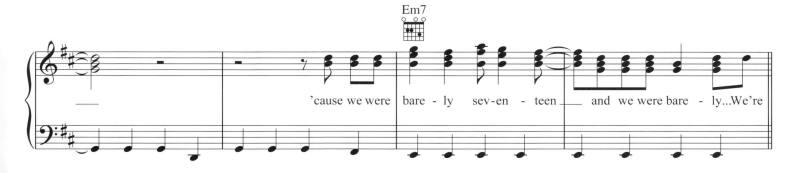

— 'cause we were bare - ly sev - en - teen — and we were bare - ly...We're

Somewhat slower, with a beat

gon - na go all — the way to-night, we're gon - na go all the way and to-night's the night. We're
gon - na go all — the way to-night, we're gon - na go all the way and to-night's the night.

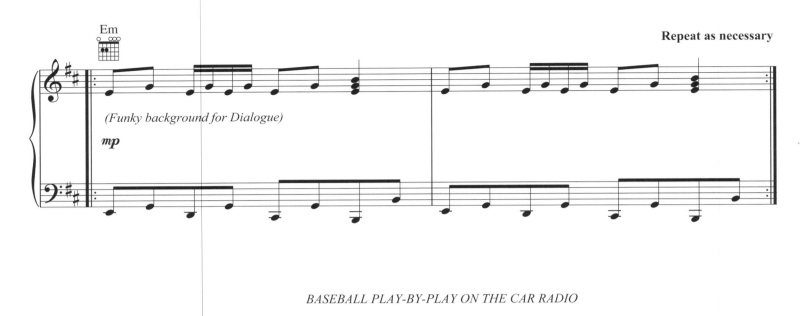

BASEBALL PLAY-BY-PLAY ON THE CAR RADIO

O.K., here we go, we got a real pressure cooker going here, two down, nobody on, no score, bottom of the ninth, there's the wind up, and there it is, a line shot up the middle, look at him go. This boy can really fly!

He's rounding first and really turning it on now, he's not letting up at all, he's gonna try for second; the ball is bobbled out in center, and here comes the throw, and what a throw! He's gonna slide in head first, here he comes, he's out! No, wait safe-safe at second base, this kid really makes things happen out there.

Batter steps up to the plate, here's the pitch–he's going, and what a jump he's got, he's trying for third, here's the throw, it's in the dirt–safe at third! Holy cow, stolen base!

He's taking a pretty big lead out there, almost daring him to try and pick him off. The pitcher glances over, winds up, and it's bunted, bunted down the third base line, the suicide squeeze is on! Here he comes, squeeze play, it's gonna be close, here's the throw, here's the play at the plate, holy cow, I think he's gonna make it!

go an-y fur-ther, do you love __ me? Will you love me for-ev - er? Do you

need me? Will you nev - er leave __ me? Will you make me so hap-py for the

rest of my life? __ Will you take me a - way __ and will you make me your wife? __ Do you

love me? Will you love me for-ev - er? Do you need __ me? Will you

nev - er leave __ me? Will you make me so hap-py for the rest of my life? __ Will you

take me a-way __ and will you make me your wife? __ I got-ta know right now.

Be-fore we go an-y fur-ther, do you love me? Will you

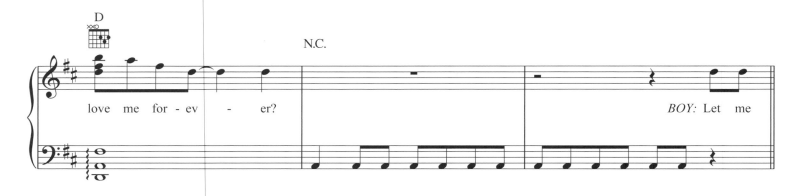

love me for-ev-er? *BOY:* Let me

sleep on __ it. __ Ba-by, ba-by, let me sleep on it. __

Let me sleep on it, __ and I'll give you an an-swer in the

morn - ing. Let me sleep on ___ it. ___

Ba - by, ba - by, let me sleep on it. ___ Let me sleep on it. ___ I'll

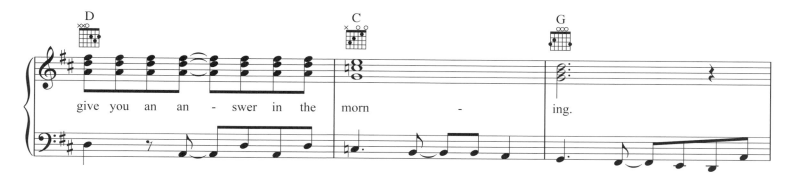

give you an an - swer in the morn - ing.

GIRL: I got - ta know right now! Do you love me? Will you

love me for - ev - er? Do you need me? Will you nev - er leave ___ me? Will you

make me so hap - py for the rest of my life? __ Will you take me a - way __ and will you

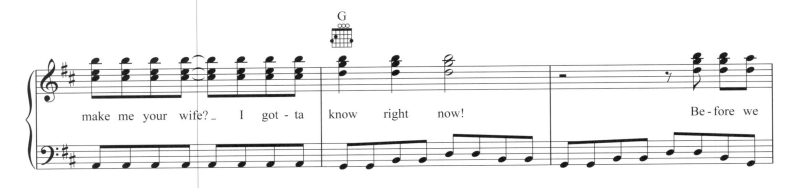

make me your wife? __ I got - ta know right now! Be - fore we

go an - y fur - ther, do you love me? Will you love me for - ev - er?

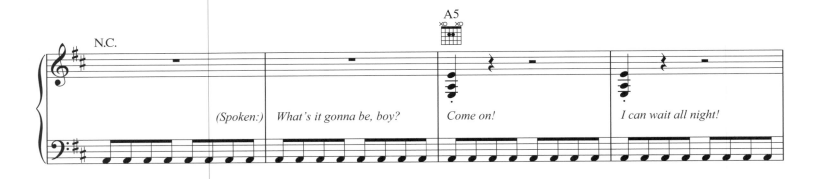

(Spoken:) What's it gonna be, boy? Come on! I can wait all night!

What's it gonna be, boy... yes or no? What's it gonna be, boy? Yes...

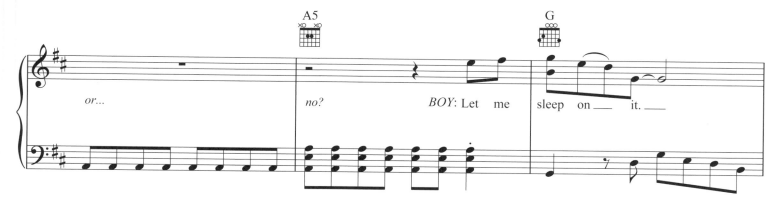

sleep on __ it. __   Let me sleep on it. __   I'll

need ____ me? __ Will you nev - er leave __ me? Will you make me so hap - py for the

give you an an - swer in the morn - ing, the morn - ing, I'll tell you in the morn - ing.

rest of my life? __ Will you take me a - way? __ Will you make me your wife? __ I got - ta

know right now!   Be - fore we go an - y fur - ther, do you

love me?   Will you love me for - ev - er?   *BOY:* Let me

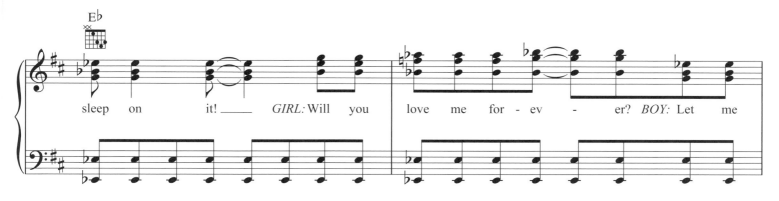

sleep on it! ___ *GIRL:* Will you love me for-ev - er? *BOY:* Let me

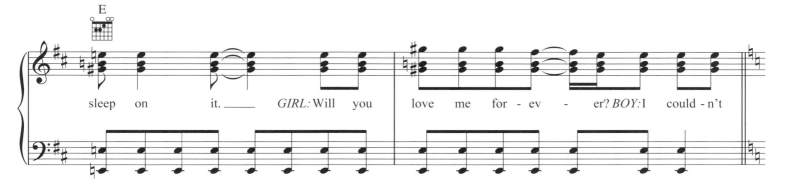

sleep on it. ___ *GIRL:* Will you love me for-ev - er? *BOY:* I could -n't

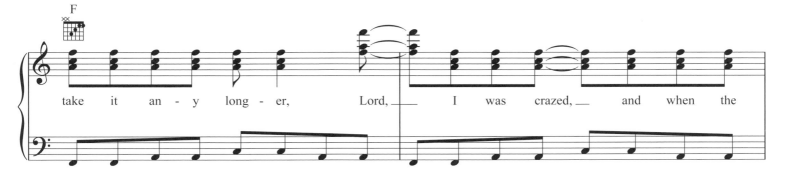

take it an - y long - er, Lord, ___ I was crazed, ___ and when the

feel - ing came up - on me like a ti - dal wave, ___ I start - ed

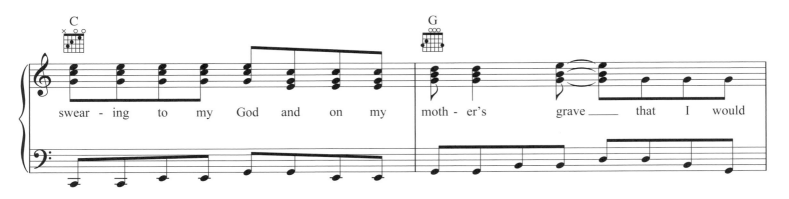

swear - ing to my God and on my moth - er's grave ___ that I would

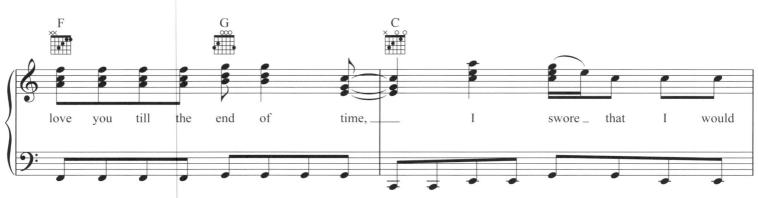

love you till the end of time, ___ I swore ___ that I would

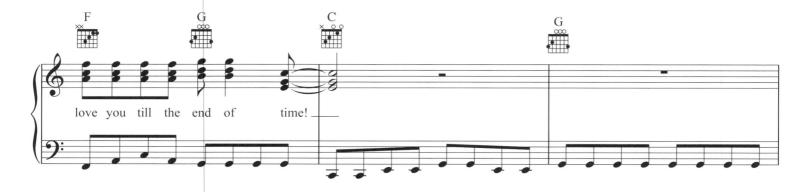

love you till the end of time! ___

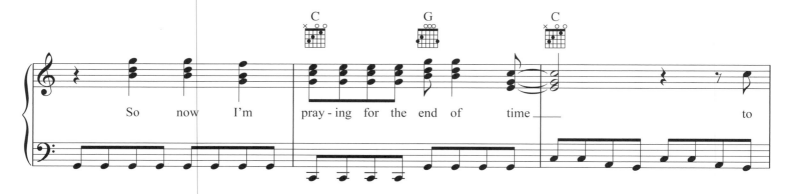

So now I'm pray - ing for the end of time ___ to

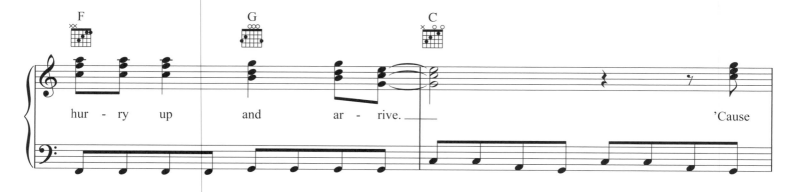

hur - ry up and ar - rive. ___ 'Cause

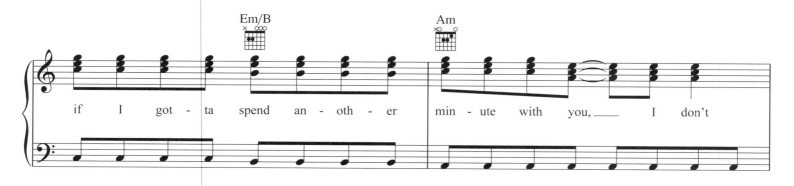

if I got - ta spend an - oth - er min - ute with you, ___ I don't

think that I can real-ly sur-vive. I'll nev-er

break my prom - ise or for - get my vow, but

God on - ly knows what I can do right now. I'm

pray-ing for the end of time, it's all that I can do.

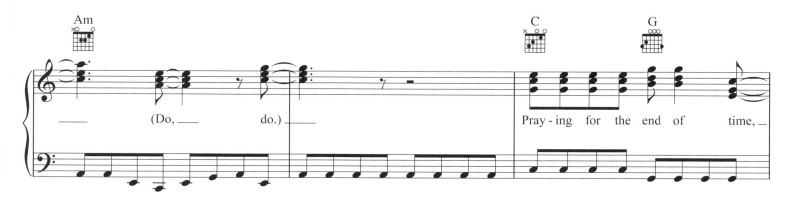

(Do, do.) Pray-ing for the end of time,

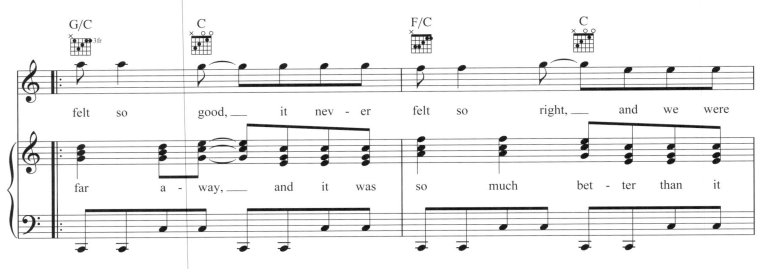

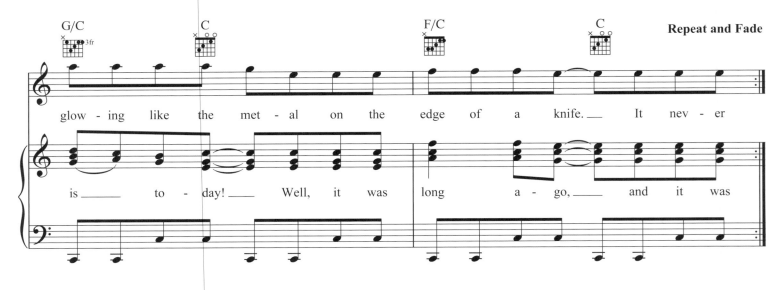

PIANO MAN

Words and Music by
BILLY JOEL

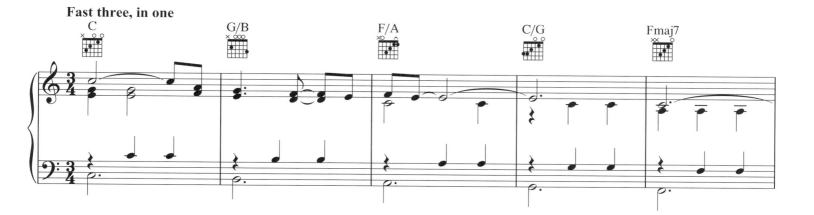

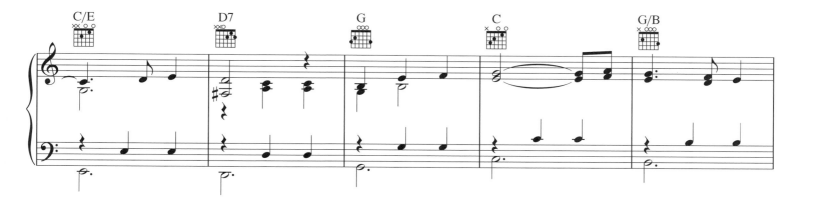

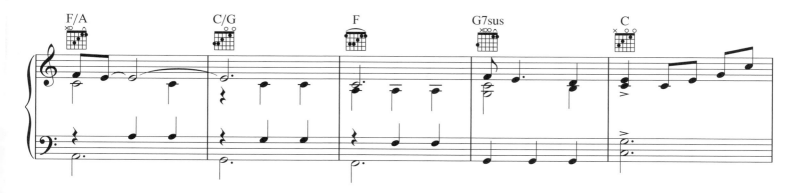

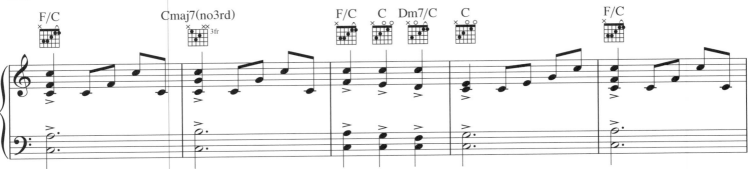

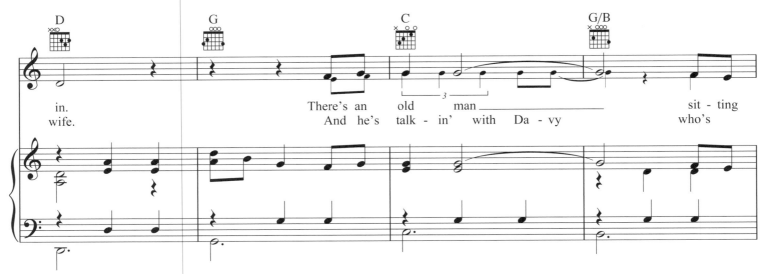

next to me / still in the Na - vy / mak - in' love / and / to his / prob - a - bly / ton - ic / will / and ___ / be / for / life. ___

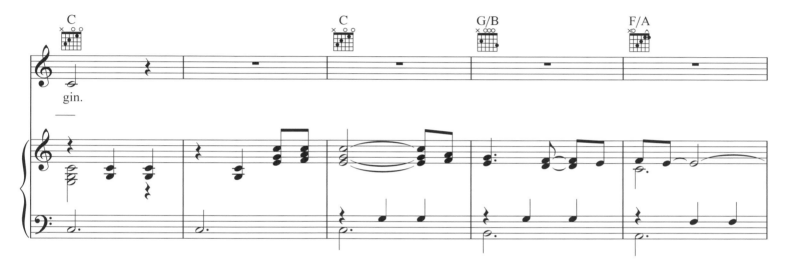

gin.

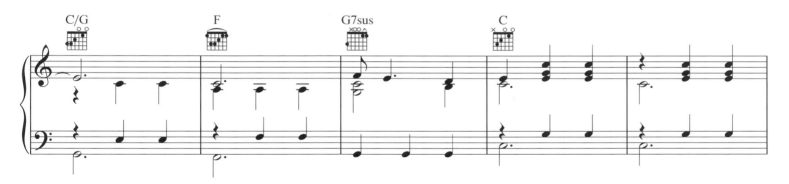

He says, "Son, can you play ___ me a / And the wait - ress is / prac - tic - ing

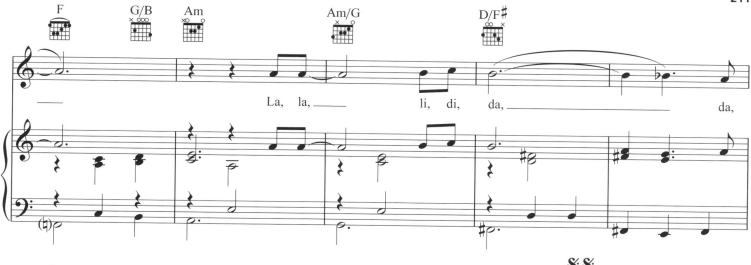

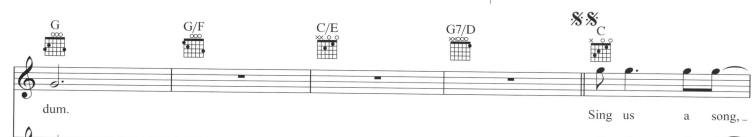

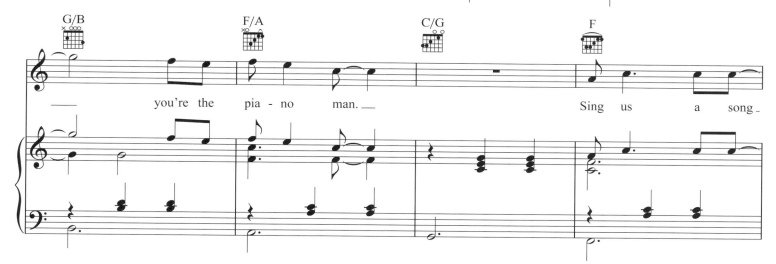

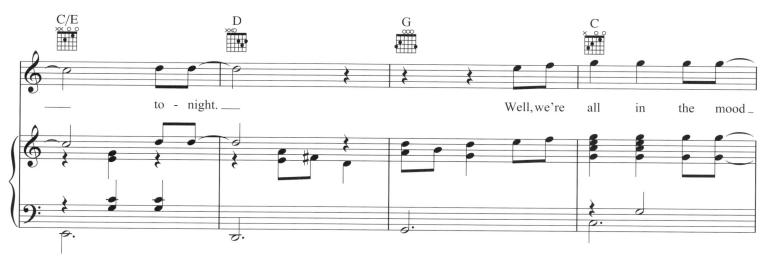

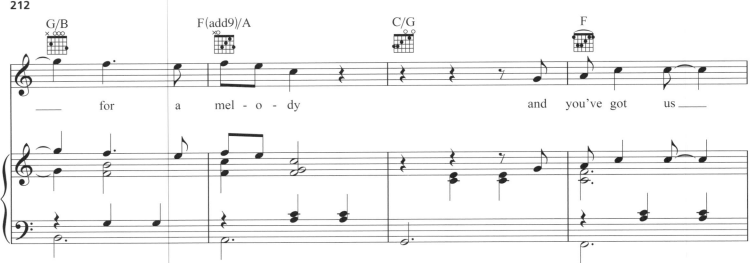

for a mel - o - dy and you've got us ____

feel - in' al - right.

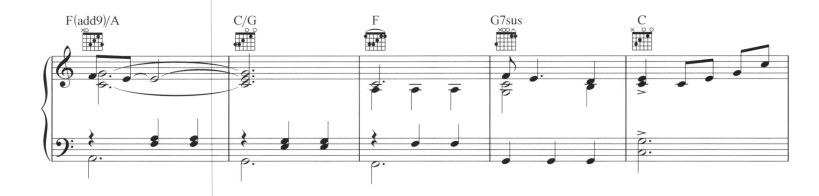

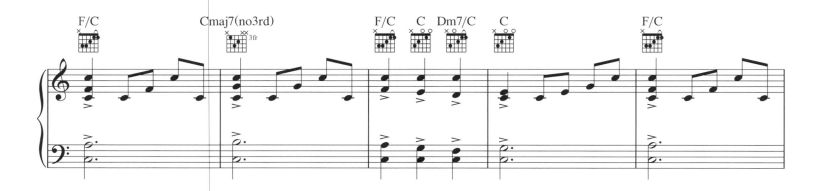

He says, "Bill, I be-lieve ___ this is

kill-ing me," as ___ a smile ran a-way from his face.

"Well, I'm sure that I could be a mov - ie star

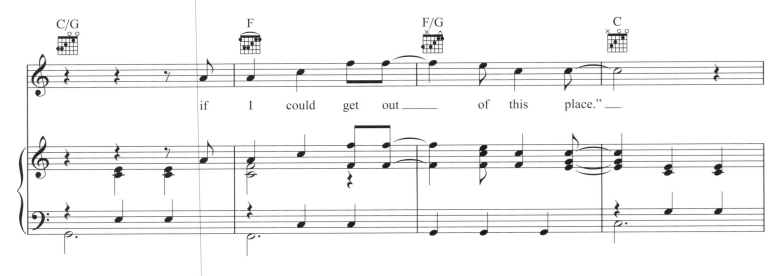

if I could get out ___ of this place." ___

Oh, __ la, la, la, __ li, di, da. ____

La, la, __ li, di, da, ____ da, dum. ____

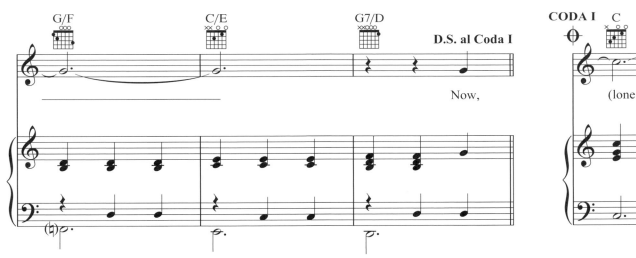

D.S. al Coda I

CODA I

____ Now, (lone.) ____

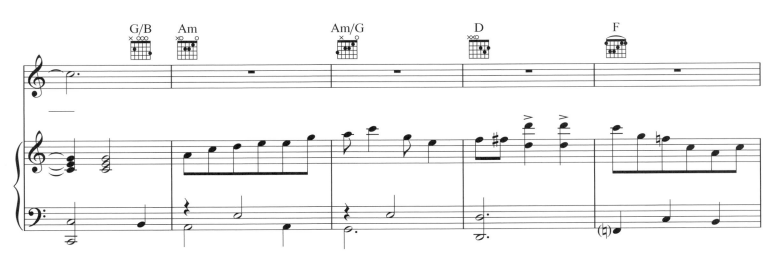

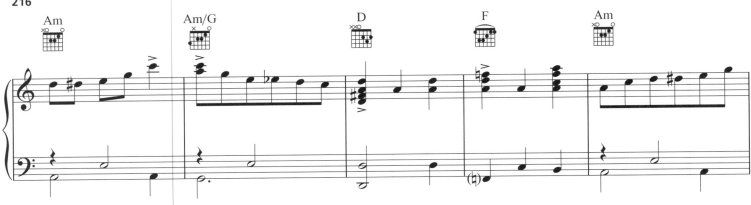

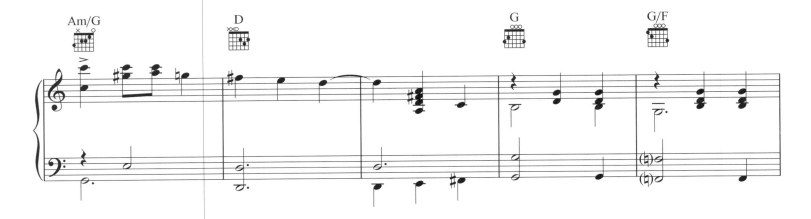

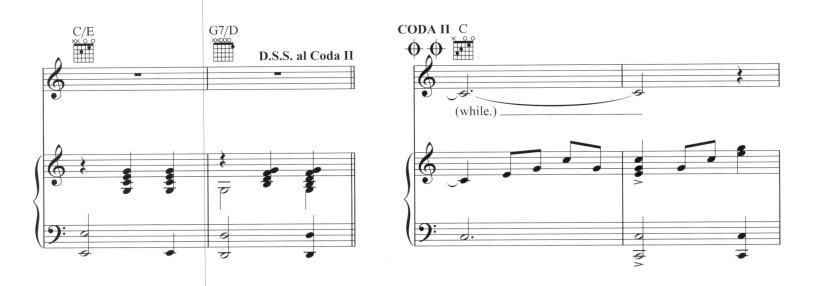

D.S.S. al Coda II

CODA II

(while.)

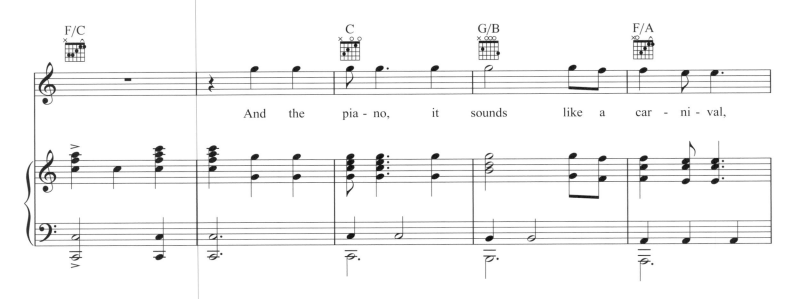

And the pia - no, it sounds like a car - ni - val,

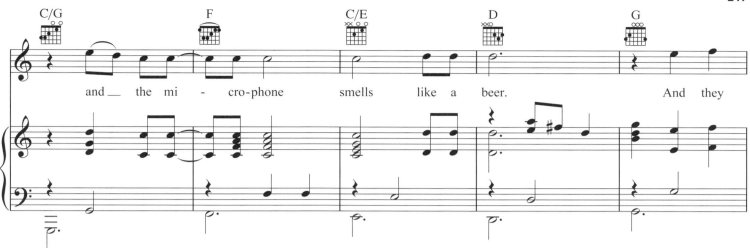

and __ the mi - cro - phone smells like a beer. And they

sit at the bar _____ and put bread in my jar, _____ and say,

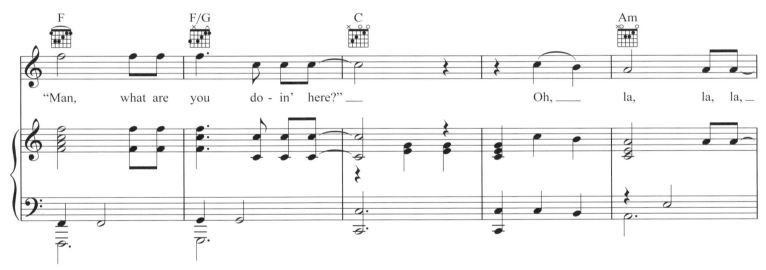

"Man, what are you do - in' here?" __ Oh, __ la, la, la, __

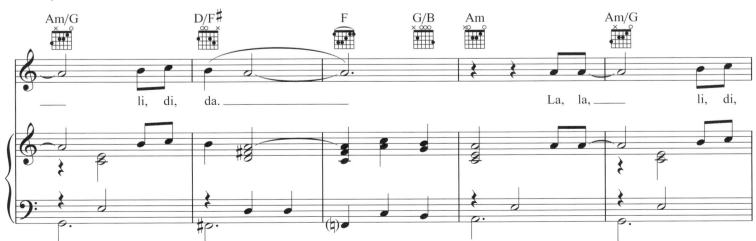

__ li, di, da. _____ La, la, __ li, di,

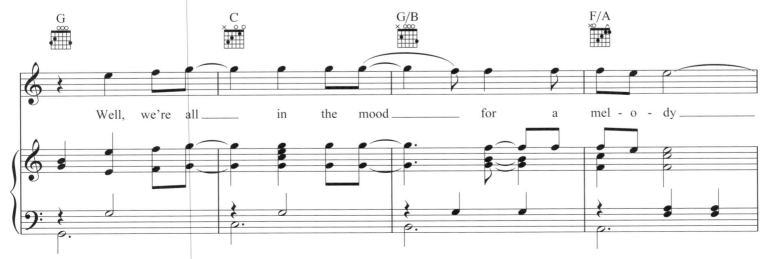

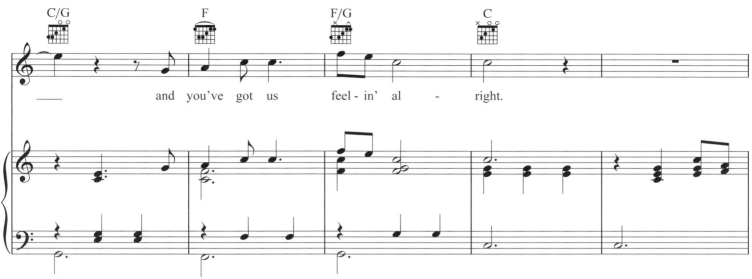

and you've got us feel-in' al - right.

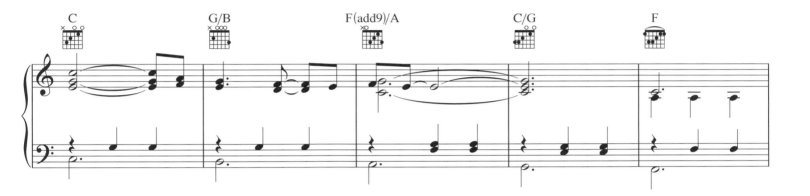

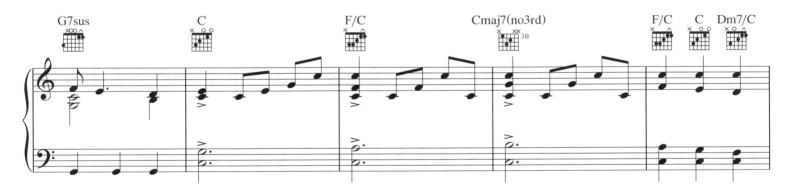

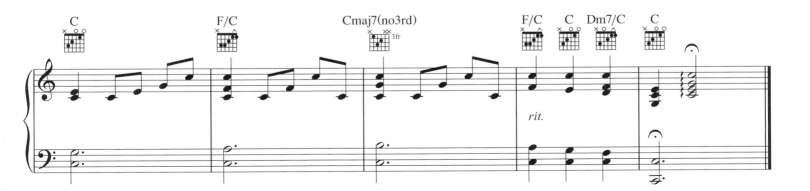

POUR SOME SUGAR ON ME

Words and Music by JOE ELLIOTT, PHIL COLLEN,
RICHARD SAVAGE, RICHARD ALLEN,
STEVE CLARK and R.J. LANGE

Break the bub - ble; _____ break it up. _____

Pour some sug-ar on ___ me, ___ ooh, _ in the name of love. Pour some sug-ar on ___ me. _

_____ C'- mon, fire me up. _ Pour your sug - ar on ___ me. _

_____ I can't get e - nough. I'm hot, stick-y sweet _ from my head to my feet, _ yeah.

Lis-ten:

from my head   to my   feet, _ yeah.

(You got   the peach - es, I ____ got   the cream.)

Sweet to taste; _ (sac - cha - rine.) _ 'Cause I'm   hot,   so hot,   stick - y sweet, _   from my
                                            (hot,   hot,   sweet, _

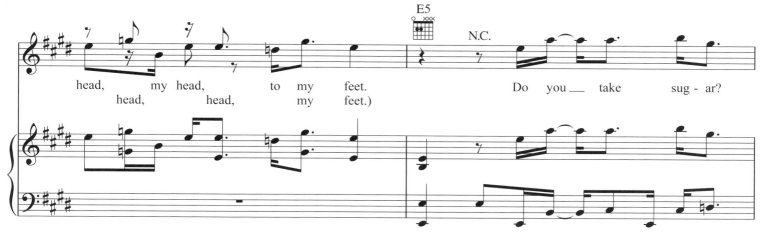

head, my head, to my feet. Do you __ take sug - ar?
head, head, head, my feet.)

One lump or two? Take a bot - tle, shake it up. _____

Break the bub - ble; _____ break it up. _____

Pour some sug - ar on __ me, __ ooh, __ in the name of love.

SHOW ME THE WAY

Words and Music by
PETER FRAMPTON

Moderately

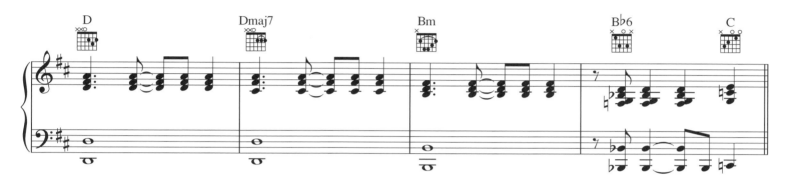

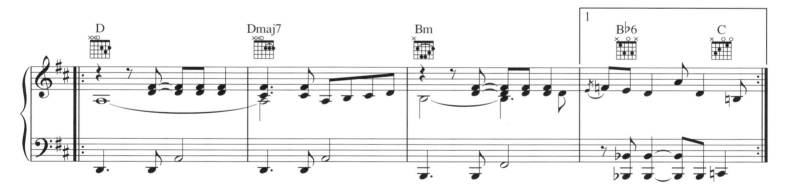

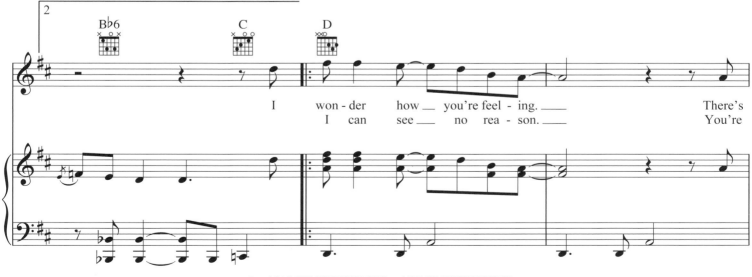

I won-der how____ you're feel - ing.____ There's
I can see____ no rea - son.____ You're

Dmaj7   Bm

ring - ing in ___ my ears, ___   and no one ___ to re - late ___
liv - ing on ___ your nerves, ___   when some - one ___ drops a cup, ___

Bb6   C

___ to ___ 'cept ___ the sea. ___
___ and I ___ sub - merge. ___   I'm

D   Dmaj7

Who can I ___ be - lieve in? ___   I'm kneel - ing on ___ the floor.
swim - ming in ___ a cir - cle; ___   I feel I'm go - ing down. ___

Bm

There has to be ___ a force;   who do ___
There has to be ___ a fool   to play ___

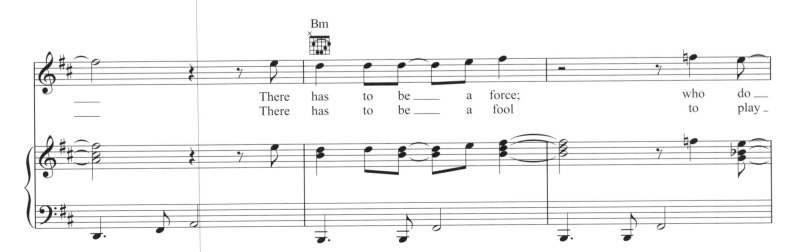

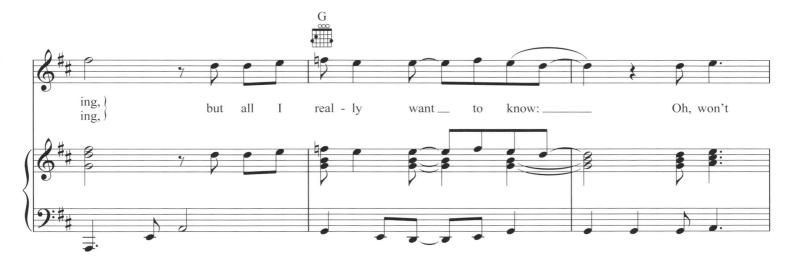

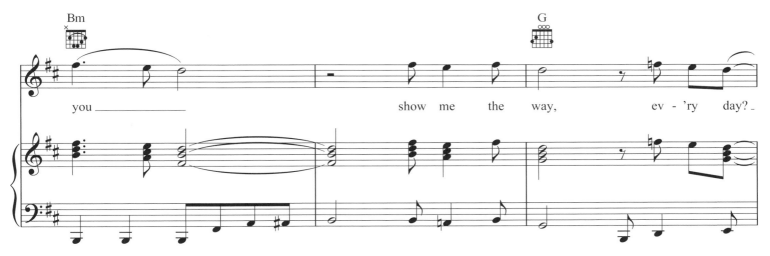

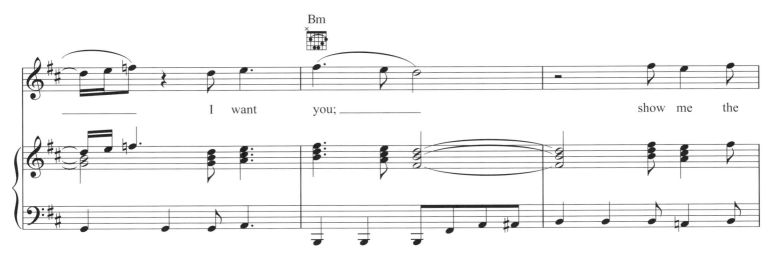

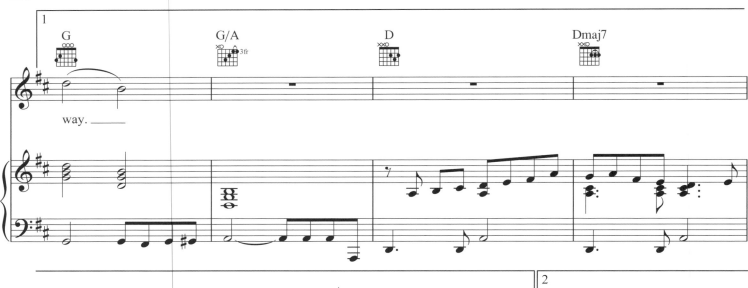

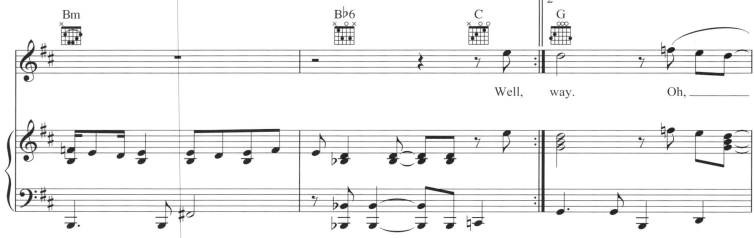

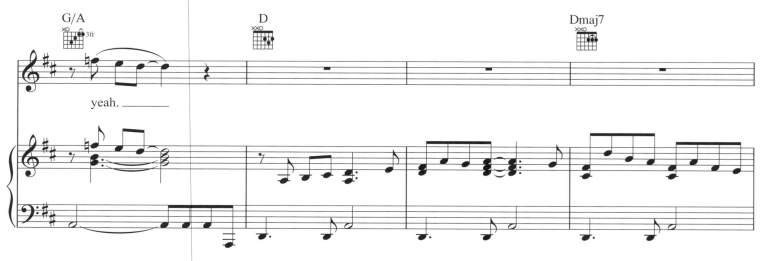

I won-der if ____ I'm dream-ing. _____

____ I feel so un - a - shamed; ____ I

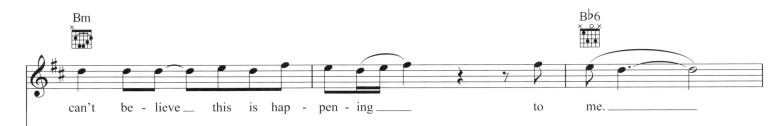

can't be-lieve ____ this is hap - pen - ing ____ to me. _____

I watch you when _ you're sleep - ing; well, then I _

_ want to take _ your love. _____ Oh, won't you _____

show me the way, ev-'ry day? _____ I want you; _____

show me the way. One more time! _____ I want

you _____ day af - ter day. _____

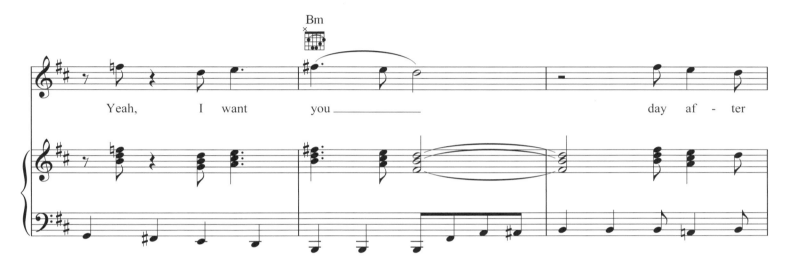

Yeah, I want you _____ day af - ter

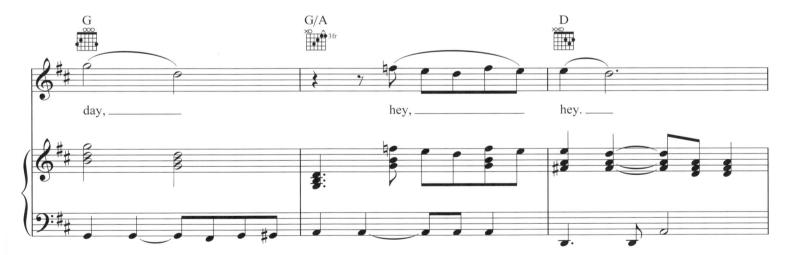

day, _____ hey, _____ hey. _____

rit.

SHE DRIVES ME CRAZY

Words and Music by DAVID STEELE
and ROLAND GIFT

Moderate Rock

I can't stop _____
I can't get _____

the way I feel. ___
an - y rest. ___

drives me cra - zy   like no one else. __

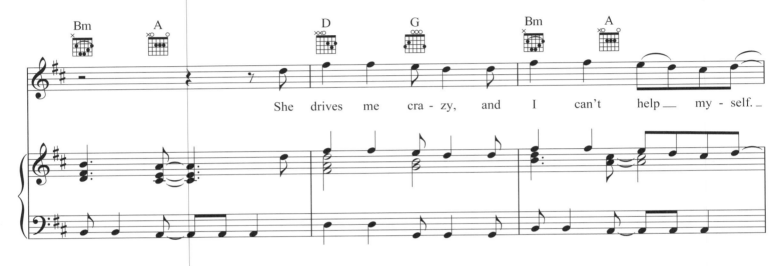

She drives me cra - zy, and I can't help __ my - self. __

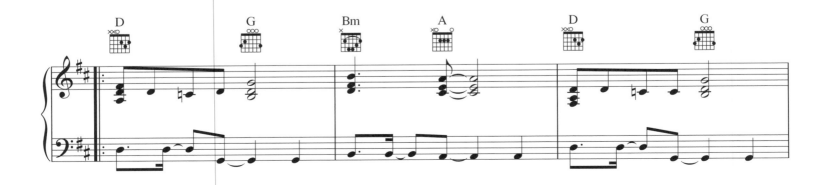

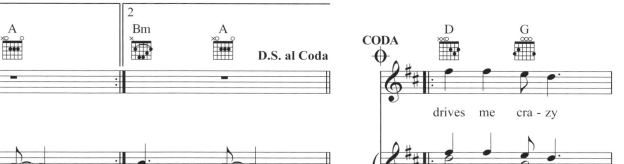

like no one else. ___ She

drives me cra-zy, and I can't help ___ my - self. ___

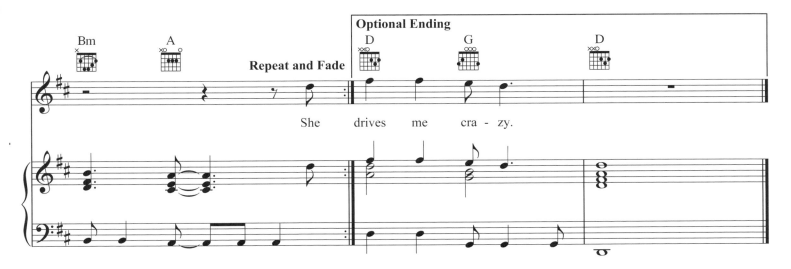

She drives me cra - zy.

SMOOTH

Words by ROB THOMAS
Music by ROB THOMAS and ITAAL SHUR

Medium Latin Rock

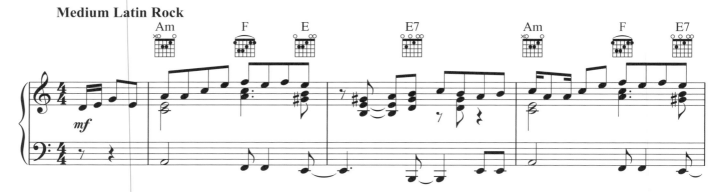

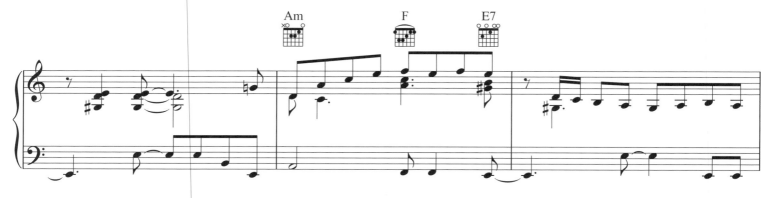

Man, it's a hot one.
one thing,

Like sev-en inch-es from the mid-day sun. ___ Well, I hear your whis-per and the
if you would leave it'd be a cry-ing shame. ___ In ev-'ry breath and ev-'ry

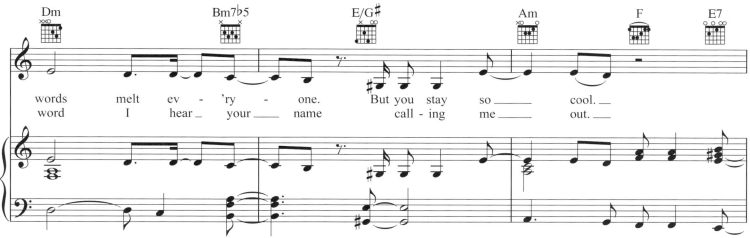

words melt ev - 'ry - one. But you stay so _____ cool. _____
word I hear _ your _ name call - ing me _____ out. _____

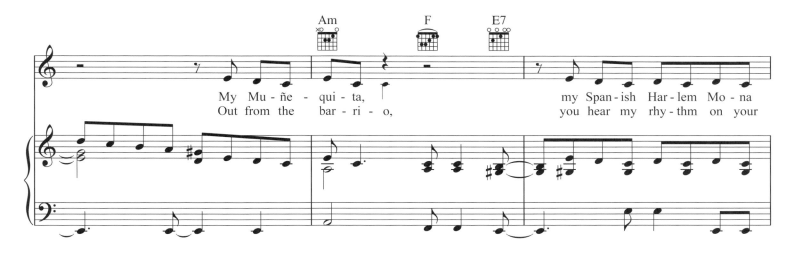

My Mu - ñe - qui - ta, my Span - ish Har - lem Mo - na
Out from the bar - ri - o, you hear my rhy - thm on your

Li - sa. Well, you're my rea - son _ for _____ rea - son, _____
ra - di - o. You feel the turn - ing of the world so soft and slow;

the _ step in my groove. _____
turn - ing me round and round. _ }

And if you said _

this life ain't good e- nough, I would give my world to

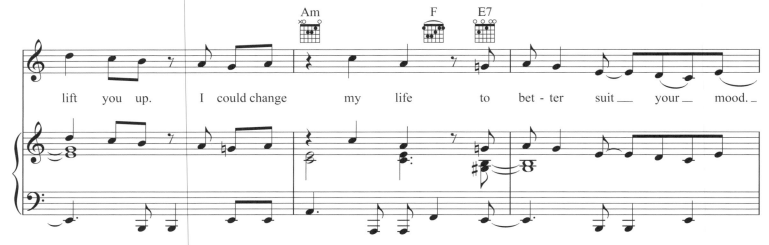

lift you up. I could change my life to bet - ter suit __ your __ mood. __

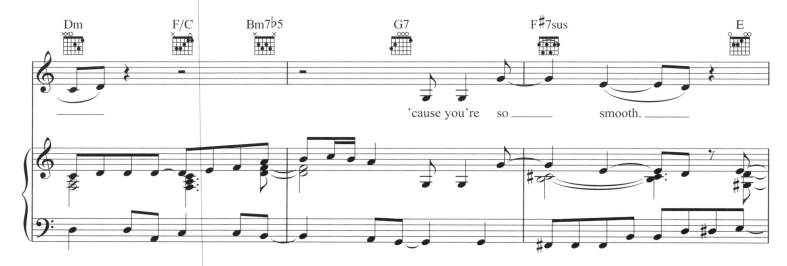

'cause you're so _____ smooth. _____

And it's just like the o - cean un - der the moon._ Well, it's the

same as the e-mo-tion that I get from you. _____ You got the kind of lov-in' that can

be so smooth, ___ Give me your heart. Make it real or else for-get a-bout it.

Well, I'll tell you

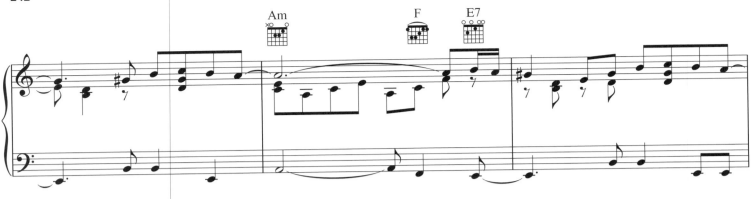

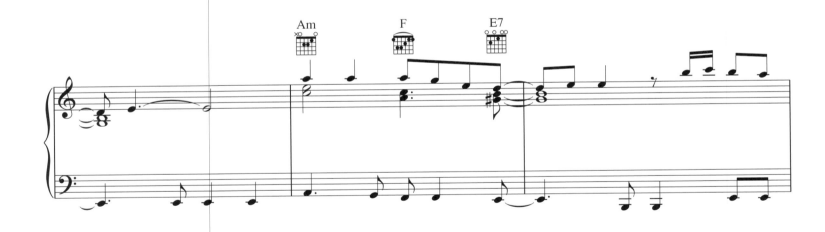

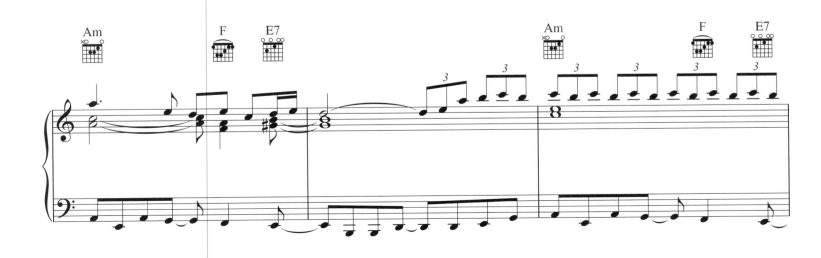

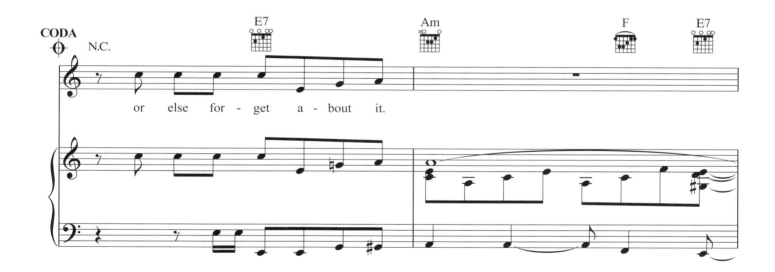

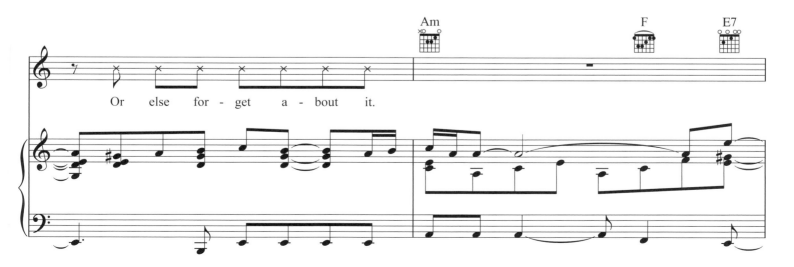

STAYIN' ALIVE

from the Motion Picture SATURDAY NIGHT FEVER

Words and Music by BARRY GIBB,
ROBIN GIBB and MAURICE GIBB

Medium Rock beat

Well, you can tell

____ by the way I use ___ my walk, I'm a wom-an's man: no time to talk. ___
____ get ___ low and I ___ get high, ___ and if I ____ can't get ei-ther, I real-ly try. ___ Got the

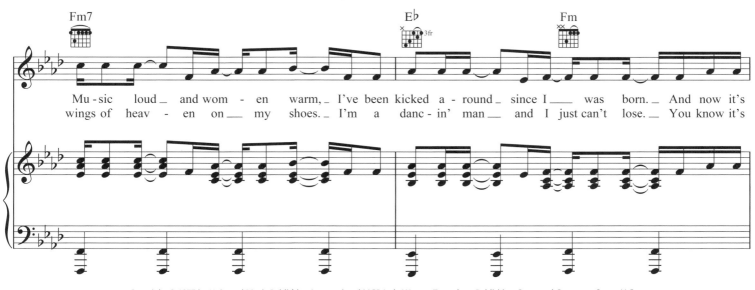

Mu-sic loud ___ and wom-en warm, ___ I've been kicked a-round ___ since I ___ was born. ___ And now it's
wings of heav-en on ___ my shoes. I'm a danc-in' man ___ and I just can't lose. You know it's

Ah, ha, ha, ha, stay-in' a - live, _ stay-in' a - live. _ Ah, ha, ha, ha,

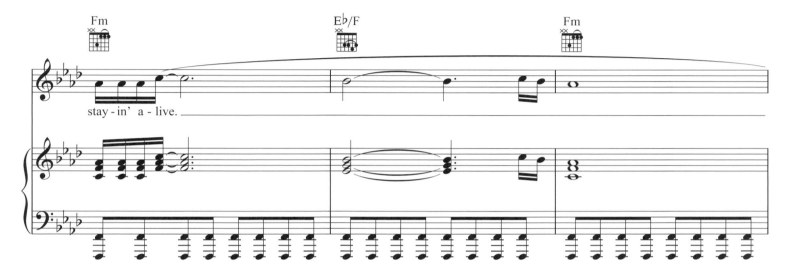

Fm   Eb/F   Fm

stay - in' a - live. _

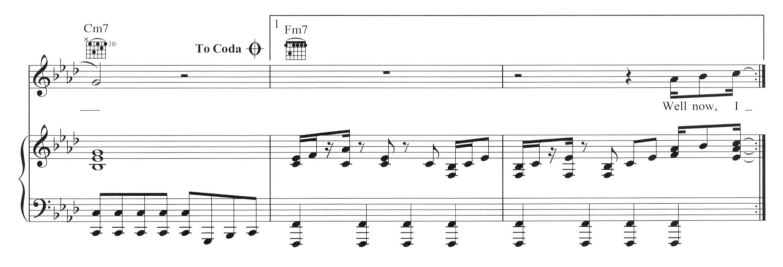

Cm7   **To Coda** ⊕ | 1. Fm7

Well now, I _

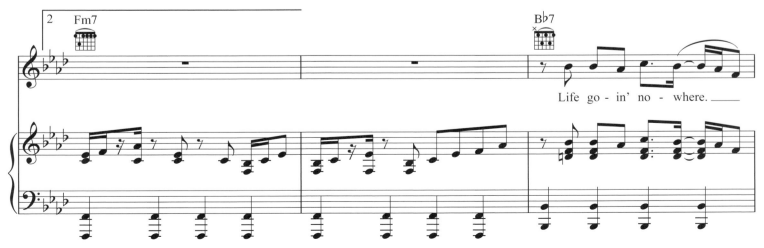

2. Fm7   Bb7

Life go - in' no - where. _____

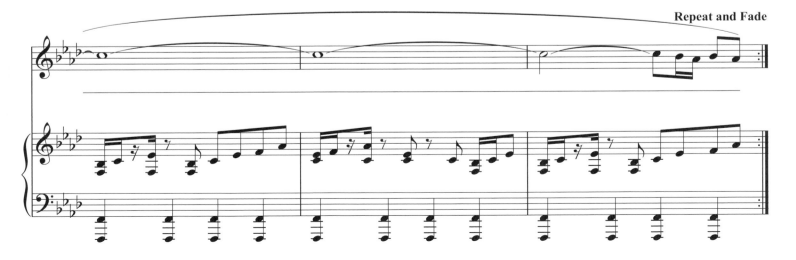

STILL THE SAME

Words and Music by
BOB SEGER

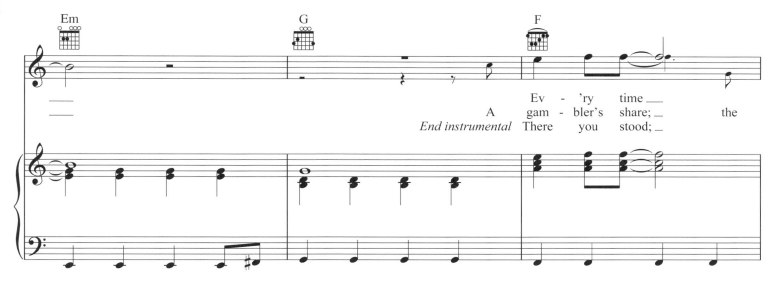

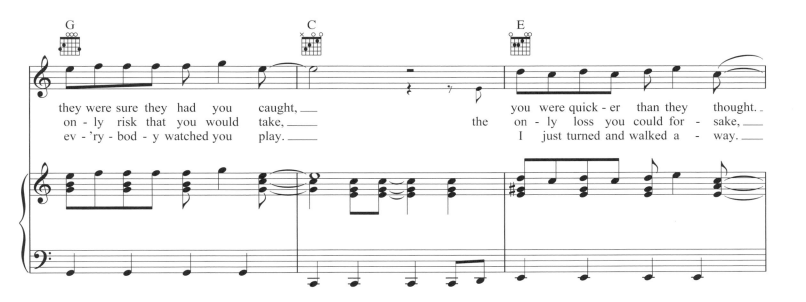

1
2

C

You

And you're still the same.

I

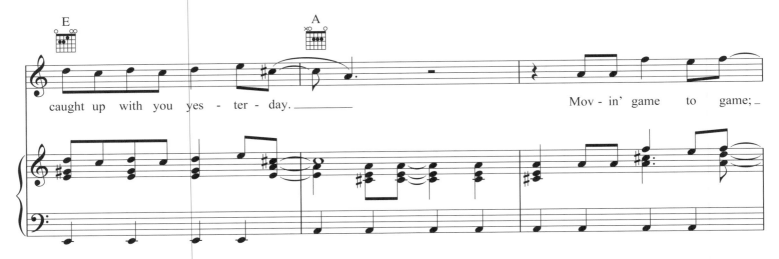

E

A

caught up with you yes - ter - day. _____

Mov - in' game to game; _

Dm

G

no one stand - in' in your way. __

C

E

Turn - in' on the charm __

long e - nough to get you by. __

And you're still the same. ___

Mov - in' game to game. ___

Some things nev - er change. ___

And you're still the same. ___

SUMMER OF '69

Words and Music by BRYAN ADAMS
and JIM VALLANCE

six - ty - nine.

Me ___ and some guys from school
Ain't ___ no use in com - plain - in' ___
And ___ now the times are chang - in'; ___

had a band ___ and we tried real hard.
when you got ___ a ___ job to do.
look at ev - 'ry - thing that's come and gone.

Jim - my quit ___ and
Spend my eve - nin's down ___
Some - times when I

Jo - dy got mar - ried; ___
___ at the drive - in, ___
play that old six - string ___

I should - a known ___ we'd nev - er get far.
and that's when I ___ met you.
I think a - bout you, won - der what ___ went wrong.

Oh, when I look back now, ___
Stand - in' on your ma - ma's porch, ___
Stand - in' on your ma - ma's porch, ___

that sum - mer seemed to
you told ___ me that you'd
you told ___ me that it'd

last for - ev - er,
wait for - ev - er.
last for - ev - er.

and ___ if ___ I had the choice, ___
Oh, ___ and when you held my hand, ___
Oh, ___ and when you held my hand, ___

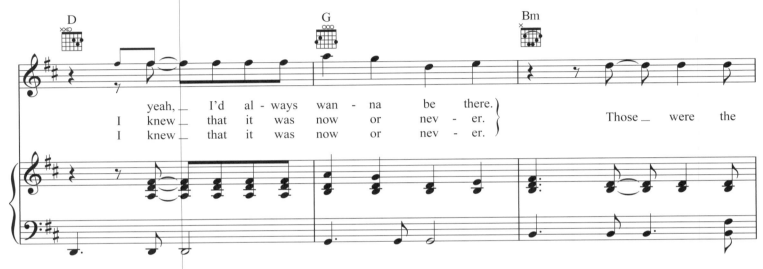

yeah, ___ I'd al - ways wan - na be there.
I knew ___ that it was now or nev - er.
I knew ___ that it was now or nev - er.

Those ___ were the

best days of my ___ life.

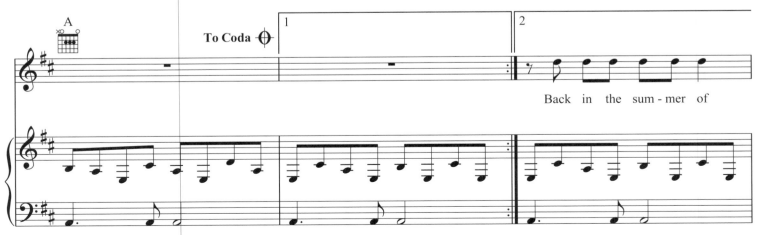

To Coda

1

2

Back in the sum - mer of

six - ty - nine. __

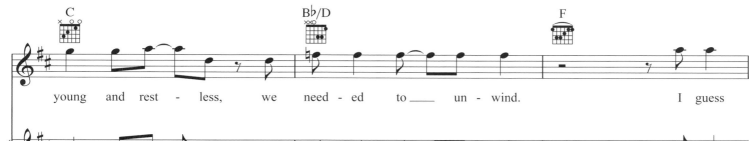

Man, __ we were kill - in' time, __ we were

young and rest - less, we need - ed to __ un - wind. I guess

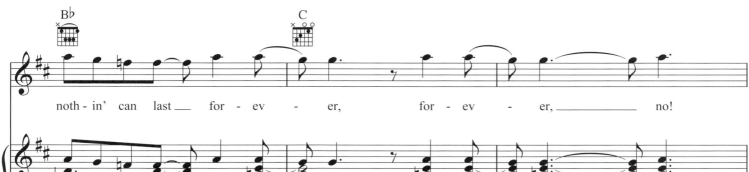

noth - in' can last __ for - ev - er, for - ev - er, __ no!

cresc.

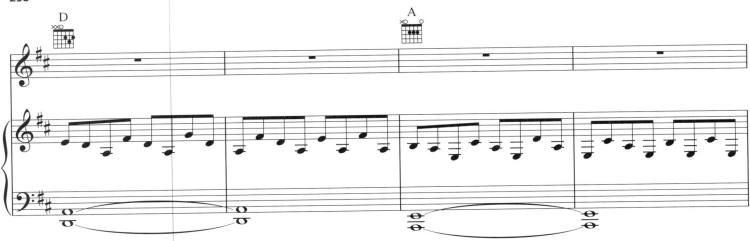

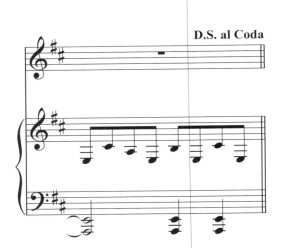

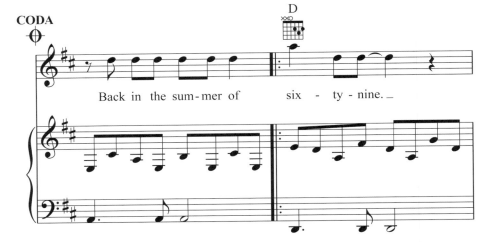

Back in the sum-mer of six - ty - nine. _

It was the sum-mer of six - ty - nine. _

UNDER THE BRIDGE

Words and Music by ANTHONY KIEDIS, FLEA,
JOHN FRUSCIANTE and CHAD SMITH

Take me to the place I love, _____ take me all the way. __

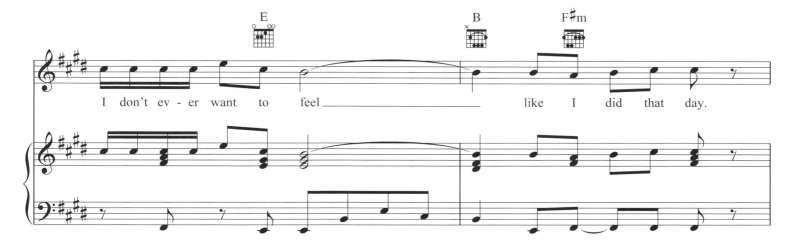

I don't ev-er want to feel _____ like I did that day.

To Coda ⊕

Take me to the place I love, _____ take me all the way, ____ yeah, __

D.S. al Coda
(take 2nd ending)

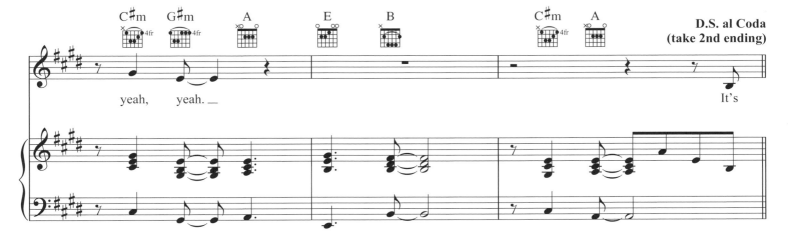

yeah, yeah. __

It's

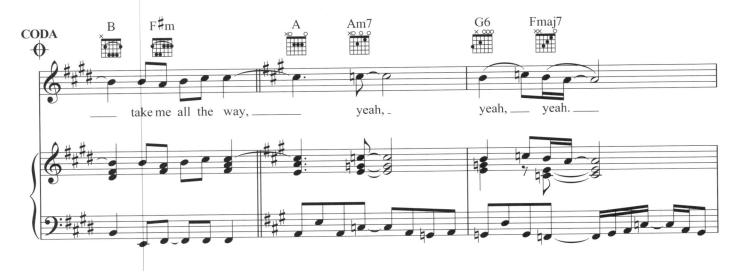

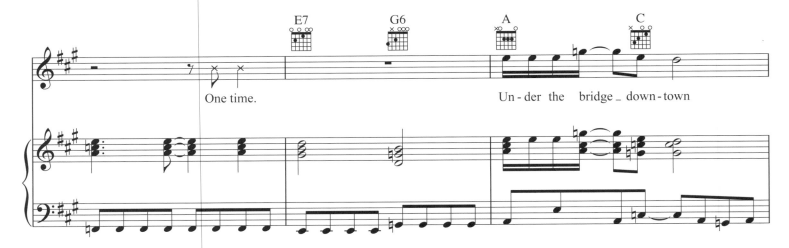

is where I drew some blood. Un-der the bridge _ down-town

I could not get e - nough. _ Un-der the bridge _ down-town

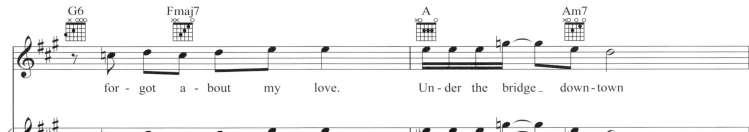

for-got a-bout my love. Un-der the bridge _ down-town

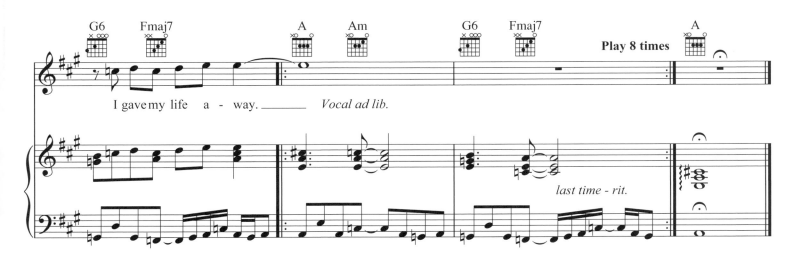

I gave my life a - way. _____ *Vocal ad lib.*

Play 8 times

last time - rit.

SWEET DREAMS
(Are Made of This)

Words and Music by ANNIE LENNOX
and DAVID STEWART

Moderately steady beat

Sweet dreams are made
Instrumental

_ of this. _ Who am _ I _ to dis - a - gree? _ I

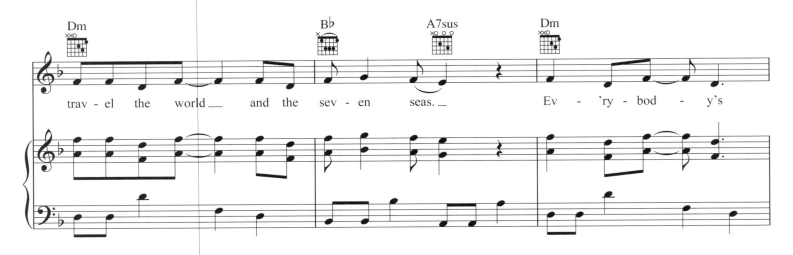

trav - el the world _ and the sev - en seas. _ Ev - 'ry - bod - y's

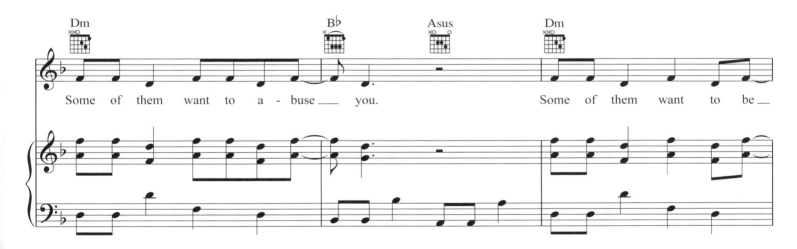

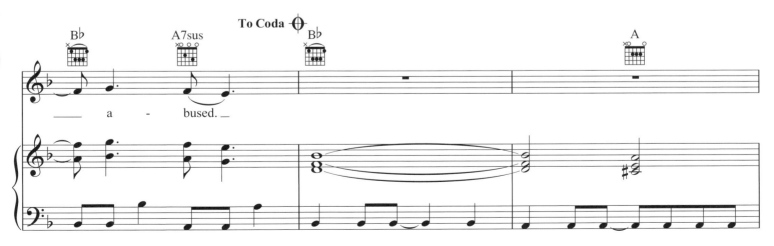

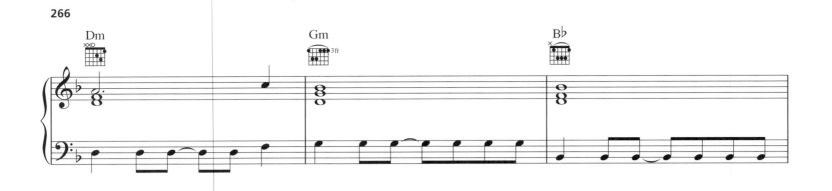

Sweet dreams are made of this. ___

Who am ___ I ___ to dis - a - gree? ___ I

trav - el the world ___ and the sev - en seas. ___

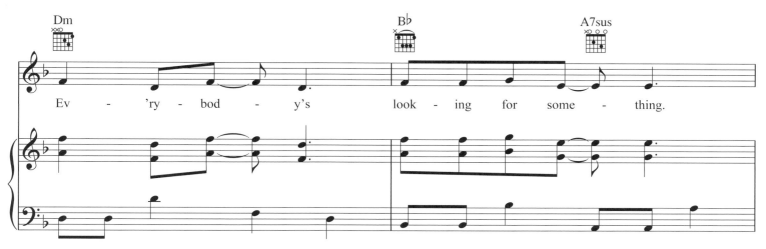

Ev - 'ry - bod - y's   look - ing for some - thing.

Hold   your   head   up.   Keep   your   head   up,   mov - in'   on. ___

Hold your head up, mov - in' on. ___ Keep your head up, mov - in' on. ___

Hold your head up, mov - in' on. ___ Keep your head up, mov - in' on. ___

Hold your head up, mov - in' on. ___ Keep your head up.

D.S. al Coda

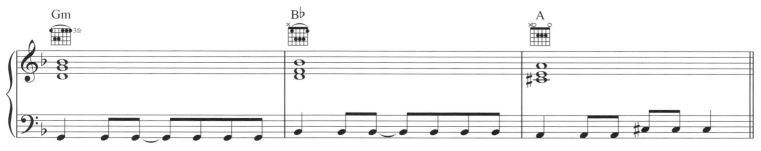

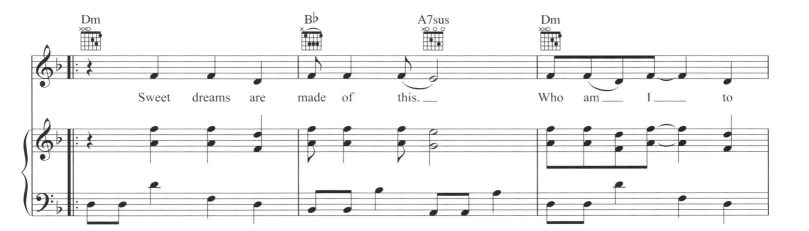

Sweet dreams are made of this. __ Who am __ I __ to

dis - a - gree? __ I trav - el the world __ and the

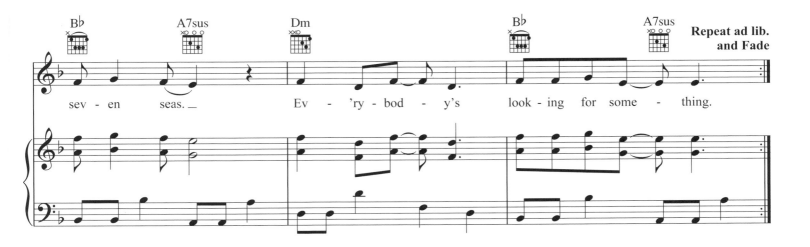

sev - en seas. __ Ev - 'ry - bod - y's look - ing for some - thing.

**Repeat ad lib.
and Fade**

TIME AFTER TIME

Words and Music by CYNDI LAUPER
and ROB HYMAN

Moderately fast Rock

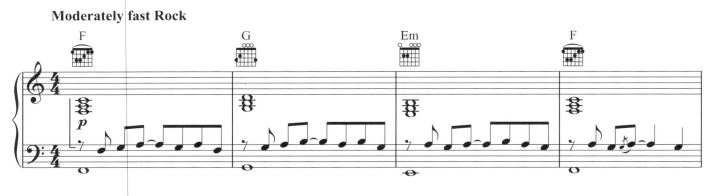

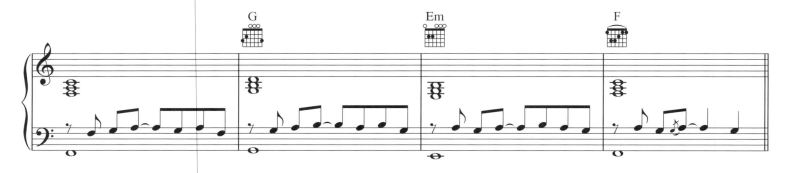

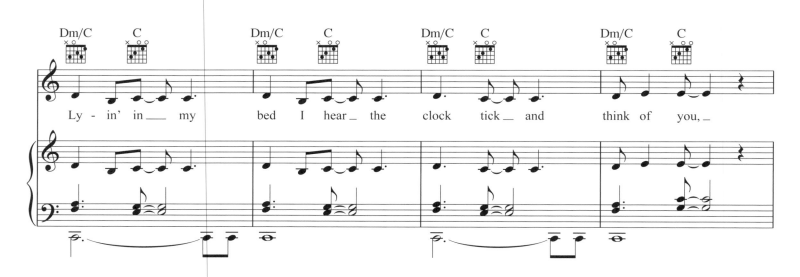

Ly - in' in __ my bed I hear __ the clock tick __ and think of you, __

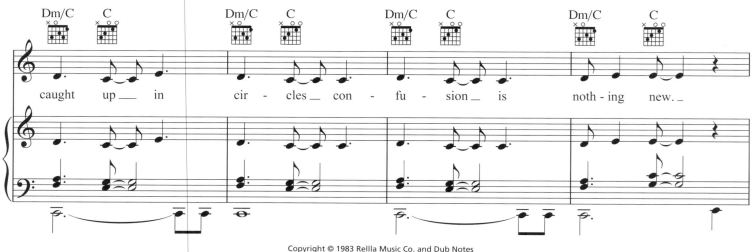

caught up __ in cir - cles __ con - fu - sion __ is noth - ing new. __

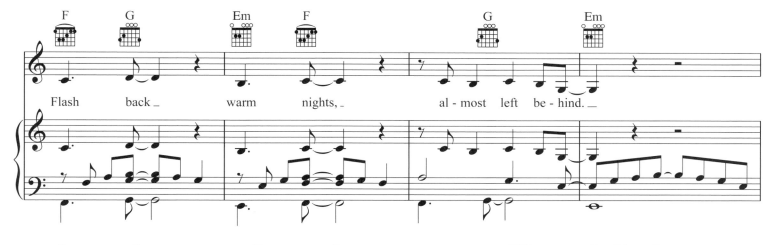

Flash back _ warm nights, _ al - most left be - hind. _

Suit - case _ of mem - o - ries _ time af - ter. Some - times _ you
After _ my

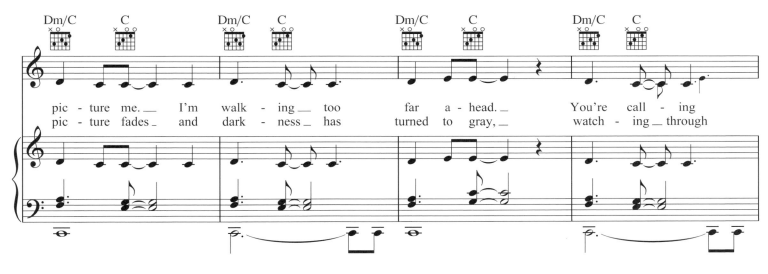

pic - ture me. _ I'm walk - ing _ too far a - head. _ You're call - ing
pic - ture fades _ and dark - ness _ has turned to gray, _ watch - ing _ through

to me, _ I can't hear _ what you've _ said. _ Then you say _
win - dows, _ you're won - der - ing _ if I'm O. K. _ Se - crets
You say _

you can look___ and you will___ find me,___ time af - ter time.___

If you fall,___ I will catch___ you; I'll be___ wait - ing,___

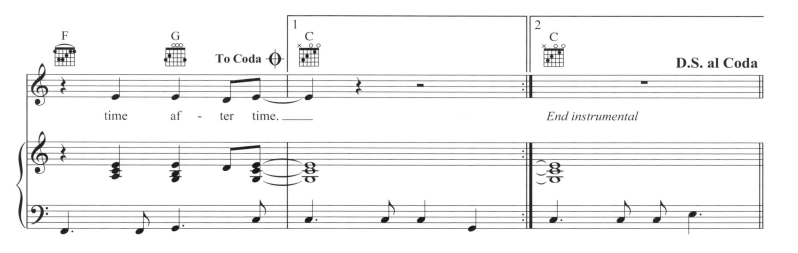

To Coda

time af - ter time._____

End instrumental

D.S. al Coda

CODA

Repeat and Fade

Time af - ter time.___

p

WAKE UP LITTLE SUSIE

Words and Music by BOUDLEAUX BRYANT
and FELICE BRYANT

Wake up, Lit - tle Su - sie, ___ wake up.

We've both been sound a - sleep; ___ wake up, ___
The mov - ie was - n't so hot, ___ it did -

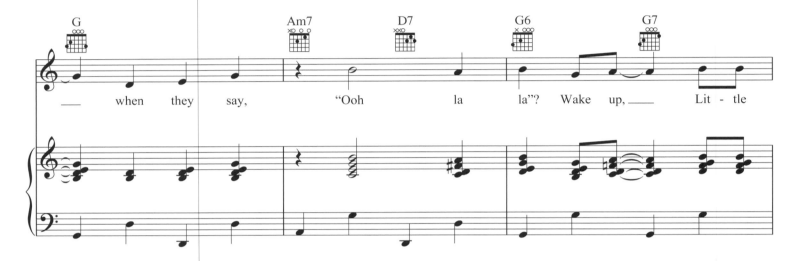

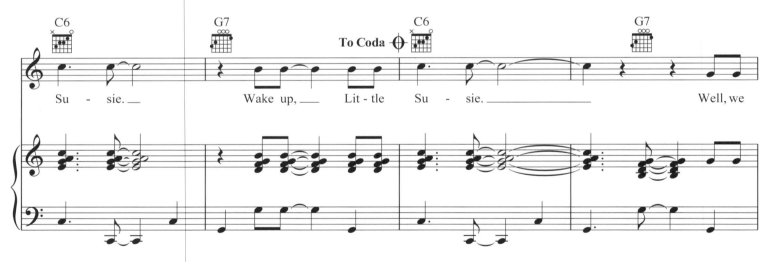

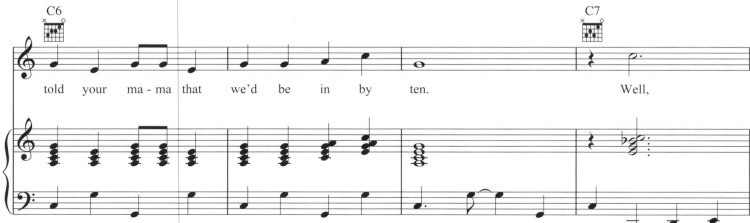

Su - sie, ba - by, looks like we goofed a - gain. _____ Wake up, ___ Lit - tle

Su - sie. ___ Wake up, ___ Lit - tle Su - sie. ___ We've got - ta go

home.

D.S. al Coda
(take 1st ending)

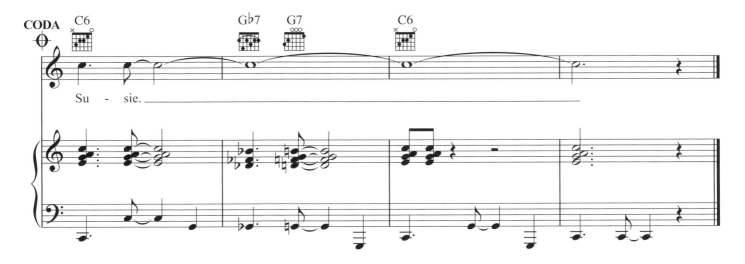

CODA

Su - sie. _____

WHAT I LIKE ABOUT YOU

Words and Music by MICHAEL SKILL,
WALLY PALAMARCHUK and JAMES MARINOS

Bright Rock

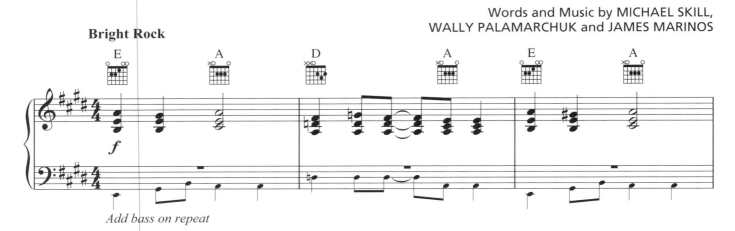

Add bass on repeat

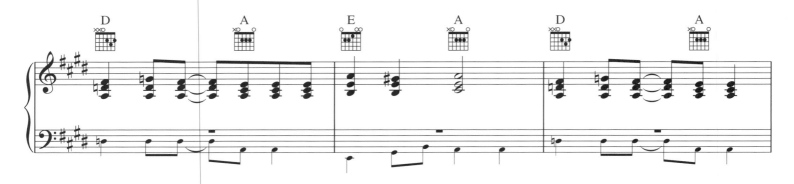

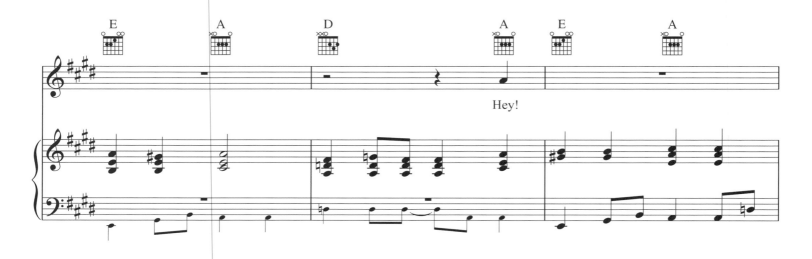

Hey!

unh - huh. _____

Hey!

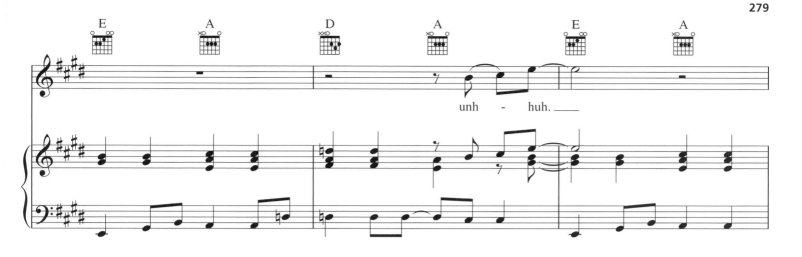

unh - huh. ____

What I like a-bout you,   you hold me tight. __
What I like a-bout you,   you keep me warm at night. __

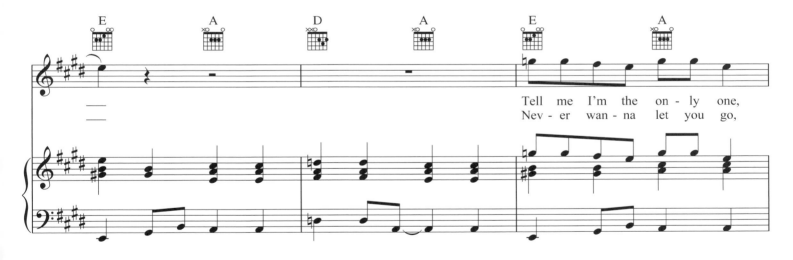

Tell me I'm the on-ly one,
Nev-er wan-na let you go,

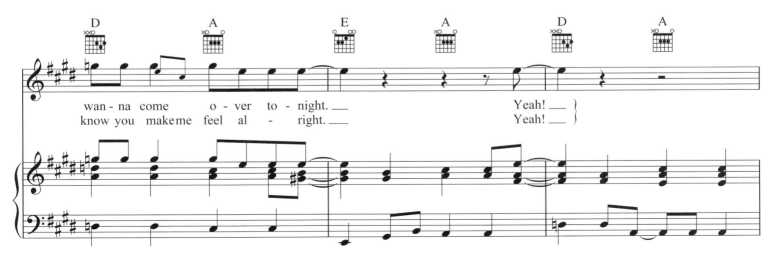

wan-na come o-ver to-night. __   Yeah! __ }
know you make me feel al - right. __   Yeah! __ }

Keep on whis - per - ing in my ear, tell me all the things that I __

__ wan - na hear, __ 'cause it's true. __ That's what I like a - bout

To Coda ⊕

you.

What I like a - bout you,
That's what I like a - bout you.

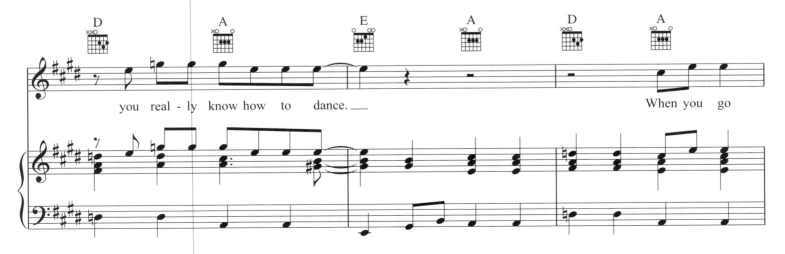

you real - ly know how to dance. __ When you go

up down,_ jump a-round_ think I've found true ro - mance.__ Yeah!_

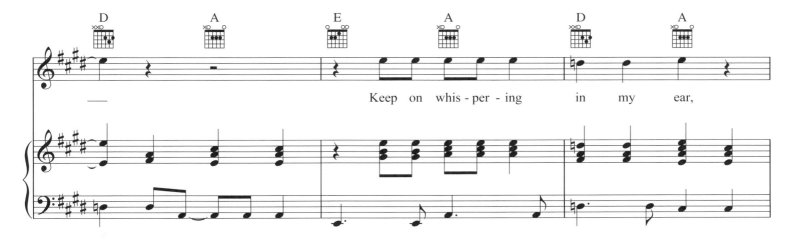

__ Keep on whis-per-ing in my ear,

tell me all the things that I_____ wan-na hear,_ 'cause it's true.__

That's what I like a-bout you. That's what I like a-bout

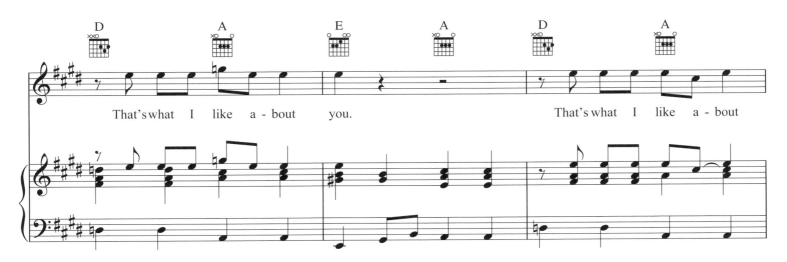

you.   That's what I like a - bout   you.

(Scream)

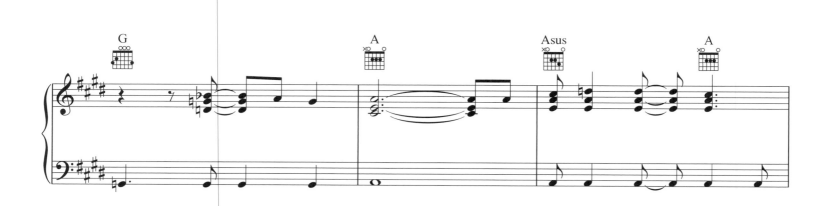

D.C. al Coda

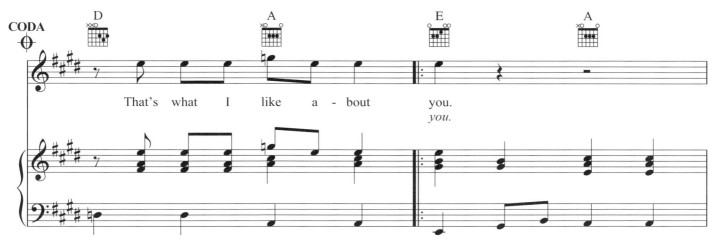

That's what I like a - bout you.
you.

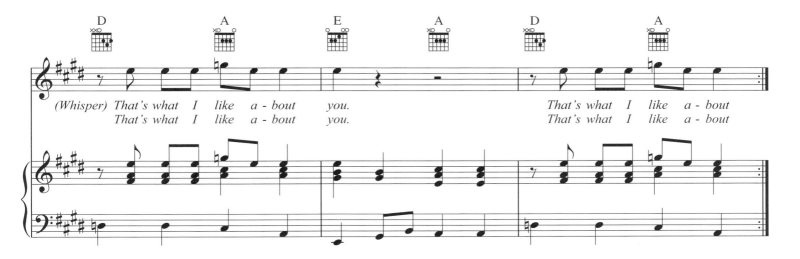

(Whisper) That's what I like a - bout you.
That's what I like a - bout you.
That's what I like a - bout
That's what I like a - bout

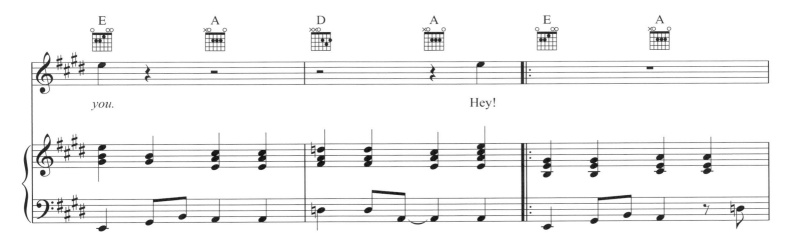

you.

Hey!

Unh - huh___ Hey!   Hey!   Hey!   Hey!

Play 3 times

WHEN DOVES CRY

Words and Music by
PRINCE

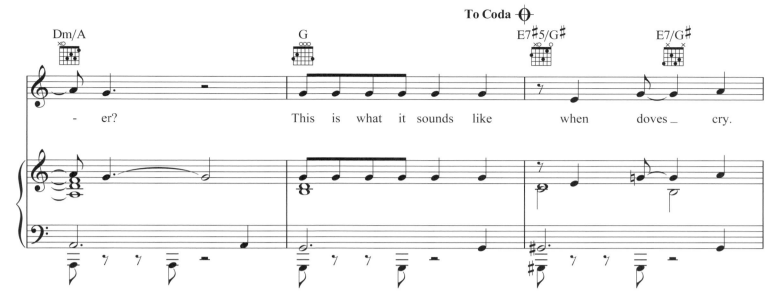

-er? This is what it sounds like when doves __ cry.

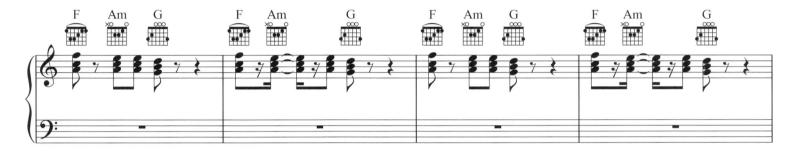

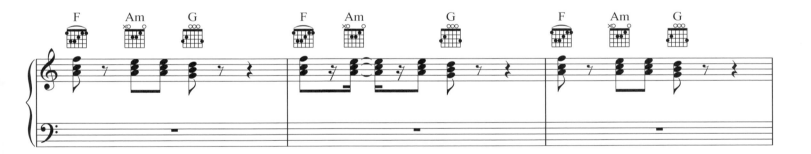

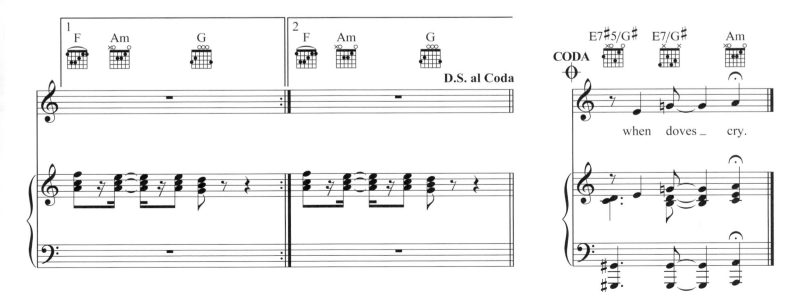

when doves __ cry.

WITH OR WITHOUT YOU

Words and Music by U2

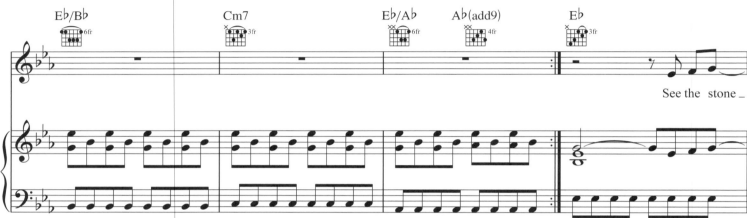

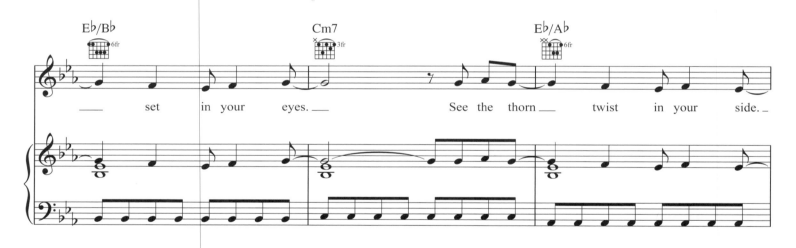

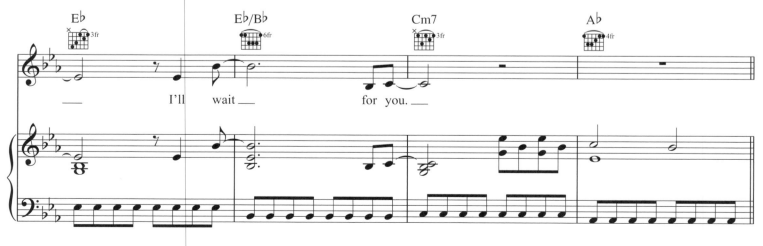

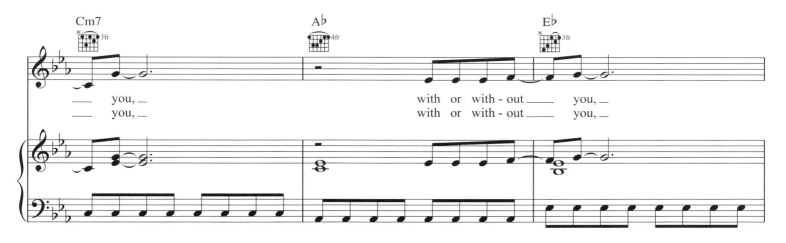

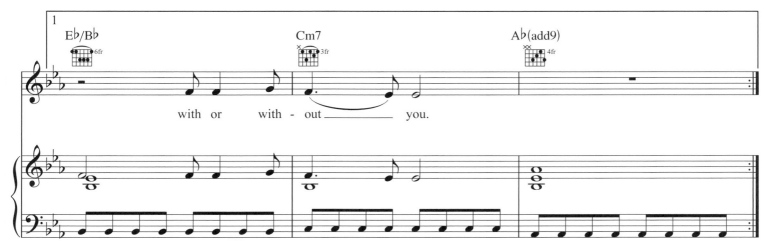

with or with - out you,— uh huh.— I can't live—

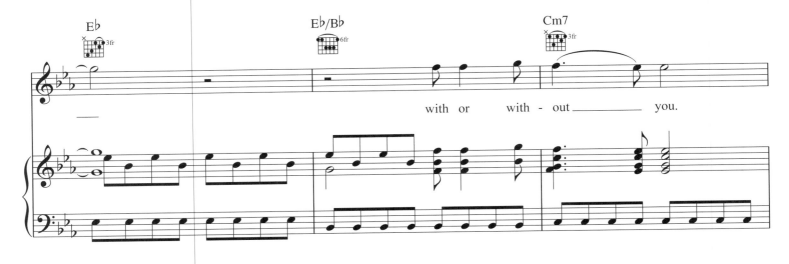

with or with - out you.

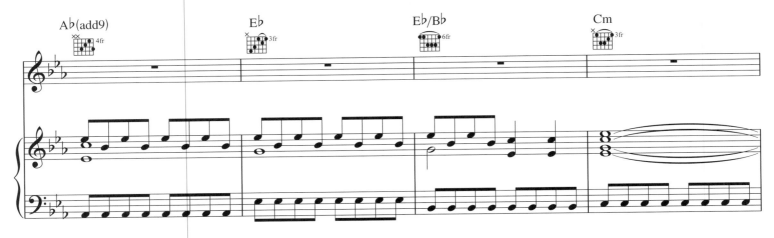

And you give your-self a - way.— And you

with or with - out _____ you, with or with-

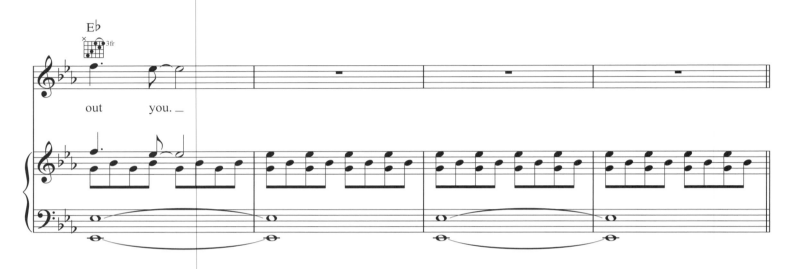

out you. ___

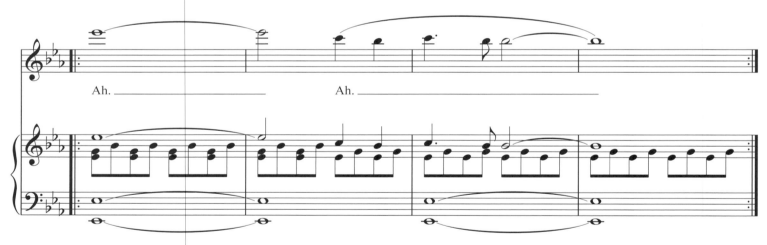

Ah. _____ Ah. _____

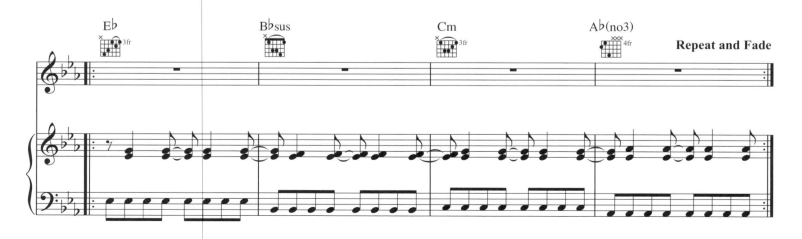

Repeat and Fade

WONDERFUL TONIGHT

Words and Music by
ERIC CLAPTON

It's late in the eve - ning;　she's won - d'ring what clothes___
We go to a par - ty,　and ev - 'ry - one turns___
It's time to go home___ now,　and I've got an ach -

___ to wear. ___　She puts on her make - up
___ to see ___　this beau - ti - ful la - dy
- ing head. ___　So I give her the car ___ keys,

and brush - es her long ___ blonde hair. ___　And then she asks ___
is walk - ing a - round ___ with me. ___　And then she asks ___
and she helps me to bed. ___　And then I tell ___

"Do I look all right?" — And I say, "Yes, you look
"Do you feel all right?" — And I say, "Yes, I feel
_____ her, as I turn out the light, ___ I say, "My dar-ling, you are

won-der - ful ___ to - night." ___
won-der - ful ___ to - night." _
won-der - ful ___ to - night. ___

___ I feel won-der-ful ___ be -

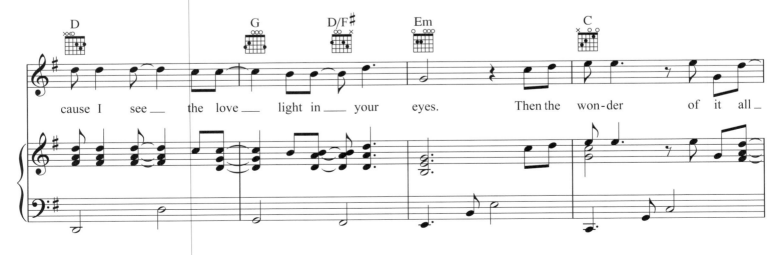

cause I see ___ the love ___ light in ___ your eyes. Then the won-der of it all _

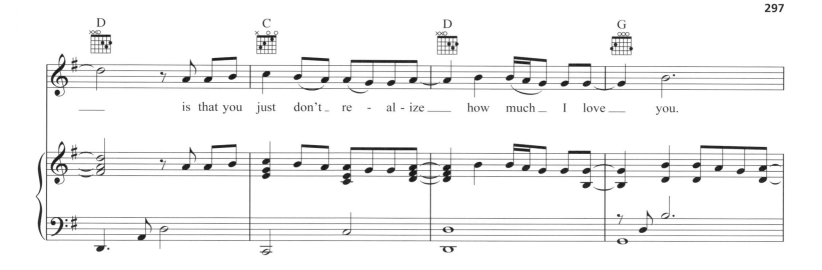

is that you just don't_ re - al - ize_ how much_ I love_ you.

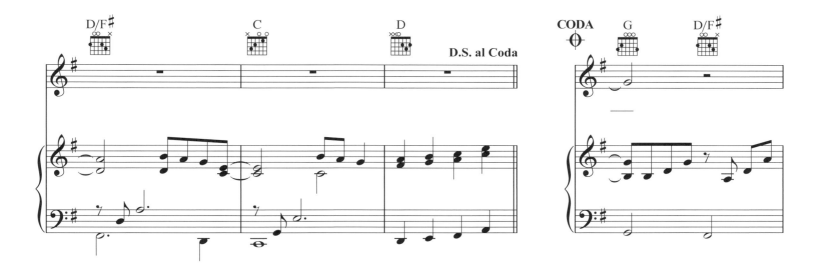

D.S. al Coda

CODA

Oh, my dar - ling, you are won - der - ful_ to - night."_

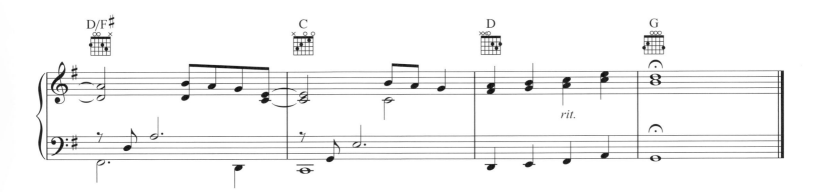

rit.

YOUR MAMA DON'T DANCE

Words and Music by JIM MESSINA
and KENNY LOGGINS

Your ma-ma don't dance and your dad-dy don't rock and roll.

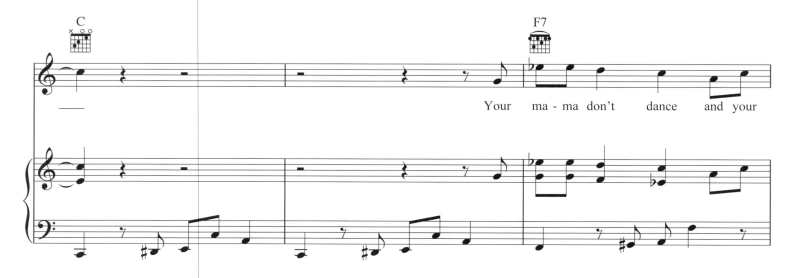

Your ma-ma don't dance and your

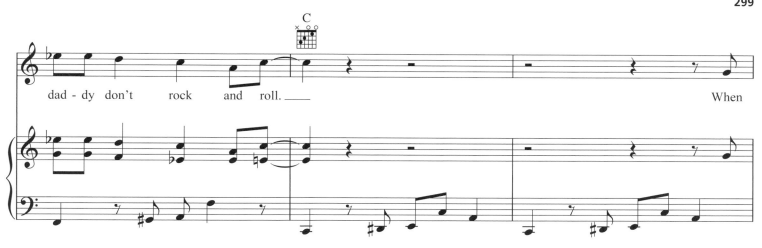

dad - dy don't rock and roll. ____ When

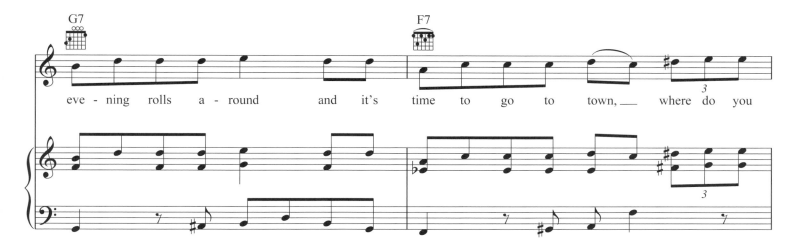

eve - ning rolls a - round and it's time to go to town, ___ where do you

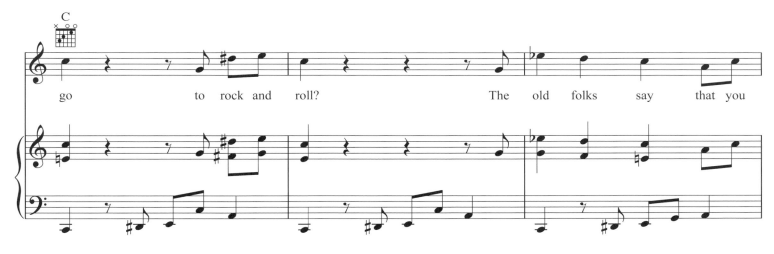

go to rock and roll? The old folks say that you

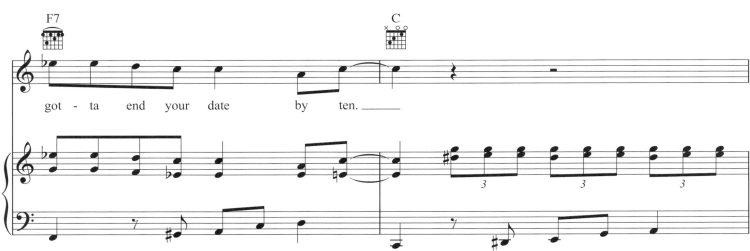

got - ta end your date by ten. _____

If you're out on a date and you

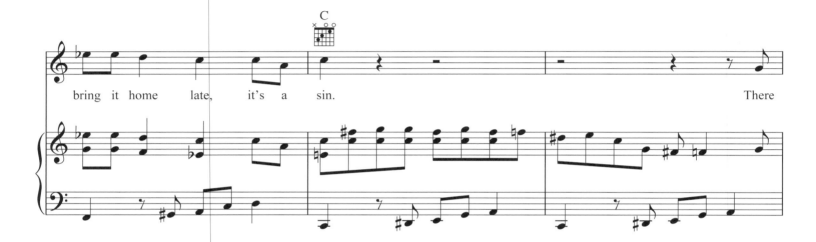

bring it home late, it's a sin. There

just ain't no ex-cuse and you know you're gon-na lose____ and nev-er win.____

I'll say it a-gain. And it's all be-cause your

(1.) ma - ma don't dance and your dad - dy don't rock and roll. __
(2.,3.) *Instrumental*

Your ma - ma don't dance and your

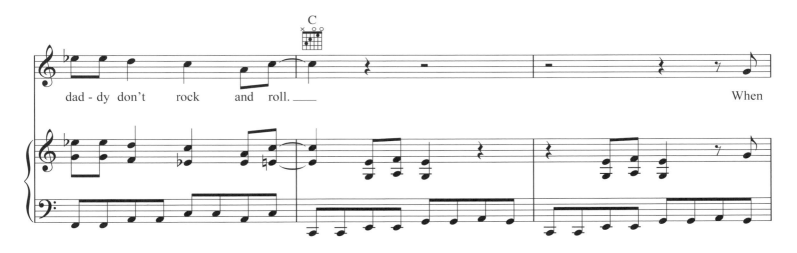

dad - dy don't rock and roll. __ When

eve - ning rolls a - round and it's time to go to town, __ where do you

go to rock and roll? *Instrumental ends* You

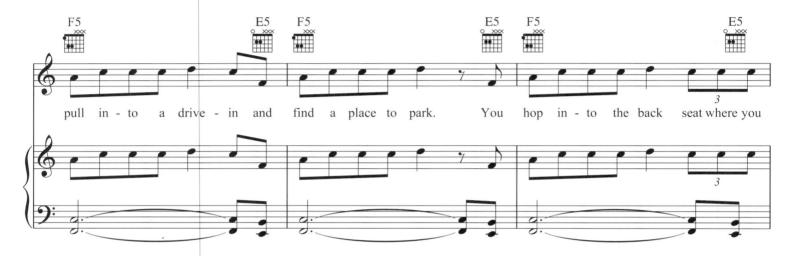

pull in-to a drive-in and find a place to park. You hop in-to the back seat where you

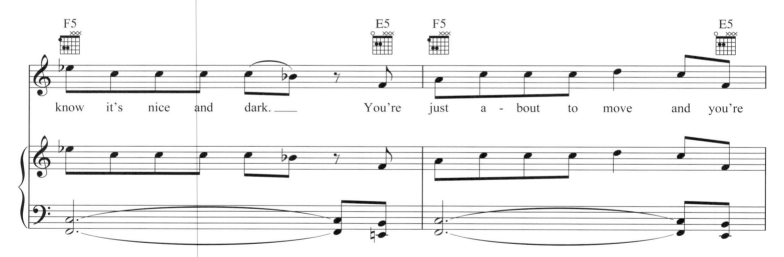

know it's nice and dark. ___ You're just a-bout to move and you're

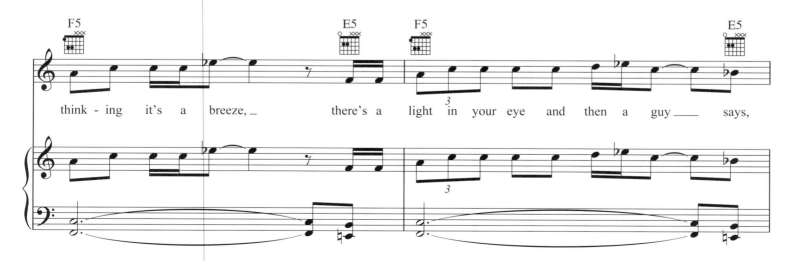

think-ing it's a breeze, _ there's a light in your eye and then a guy ___ says,

"Out of the car, long hair!" Ooh - whee! ___ "You're com - ing with

me!" The lo - cal po - lice! And it's all be - cause your

ma - ma don't dance and your dad - dy don't rock and roll. ___

Your ma - ma don't dance and your dad - dy don't rock and roll. __

When eve-ning rolls a-round and it's time to go to town,_ where do you go to rock and roll? Where do you go to rock and roll? Where do you go to rock and roll? roll?